PAGAN
BABIES

PAGAN BABIES

and Other Catholic Memories

Gina Cascone

WASHINGTON SQUARE PRESS

New York London Toronto Sydney Singapore

WASHINGTON SQUARE PRESS
1230 Avenue of the Americas
New York, NY 10020

ISBN: 0-7434-5327-1

First Washington Square Press trade paperback printing May 2003

10 9 8 7 6 5 4 3 2 1

WASHINGTON SQUARE PRESS and colophon are
registered trademarks of Simon & Schuster, Inc.

Manufactured in the United States of America

For information regarding special discounts for bulk purchases,
please contact Simon & Schuster Special Sales at 1-800-456-6798
or business@simonandschuster.com

for Roger
who told me so

Contents

≈

1. Catholic Kids Make Great Faces | 1

2. Creatures of Habit | 12

3. Don't Drink the Holy Water | 18

4. Bless Me, Father, for I Am Sinning | 25

5. Ashes and Sackcloth | 32

6. How to Get Holy Communion off
the Roof of Your Mouth | 38

7. All Things Considered, I'd Rather Be in Limbo | 44

8. Pagan Babies | 52

9. Holy Propaganda | 58

10. Martyrmania | 64

11. How Do You Know You've Been Blessed
with a Baby and Other Religious Questions
the Nuns Wouldn't Answer | 70

12. The Rosary in under Fifteen Minutes | 78

13. The Dashboard Navigator | 85

14. Get a Piece of the Pope | 91

15. What Do You Buy a Nun for Christmas? | 96

16. What Did You Give Up for Lent? | 104

17. The May Crowning | 110

18. Sister Was Not Impressed When She Found Me
Reading *The Confessions of Saint Augustine* | 115

19. The Pink Slip from the Rome Office | 123

20. The Pilgrimage | 128

21. "Don't Forget to Say a Prayer for Me!" | 131

This Certificate

IS AWARDED TO

GINA CASCONE

In Testimony of an Offering made to the *Pontifical Association of the Holy Childhood* for the *Adoption of a PAGAN BABY* who will receive the Name of

DIANE

in *Holy Baptism*

FOR THE ASSOCIATION

Augustus O. Keiter U.Bp.
NATIONAL DIRECTOR

Emmund A. Monahan
DIOCESAN DIRECTOR

DATE ___ JUN 1961

Chapter 1

∾

Catholic Kids
Make Great Faces

I WENT TO Catholic school under protest. On my very first day, my parents had to get me out of the closet twice, pull me out from under the bed by my feet three times, and retrieve me from behind the sofa. Before I could escape again, my mother had my hand in a viselike grip and was leading me down the street.

We passed the Rosellis' little brick house and heard Mrs. Roselli's opera records playing. As usual, she was singing along at the top of her lungs, though her voice was hardly as steady as Caruso's.

After the Rosellis', my mother and I both walked off the sidewalk to dogleg the Santinis' house. Their house was the only one on the block that didn't have grass growing between the sidewalk and the curb. That was because everybody walked there. The Santinis' house had a four-foot-high hedge surrounding it. Their son Pauli was usually hiding behind that hedge, ready to get an innocent passerby with a water balloon, spitball, snowball, pile of leaves, or whatever seasonable prop might be available. Even when people knew that Pauli wasn't home, they walked as far away from the hedge as they could get. It was best just to stay in the habit.

Pauli wasn't behind the hedge this morning. He wasn't even awake yet, since he went to public school and didn't have to be there for another hour and a half. The nuns had kept Pauli long enough for him to make his first communion. They then felt that they had fulfilled their duty to him and asked his parents to remove him from Catholic school. He was going to third grade at Franklin Public School three blocks away. If I ever got up the courage to actually talk to Pauli, I'd ask him exactly what he did to get out.

Appearing at the corner were another mother and child. I took heart. At least I wasn't alone in this. My mother noticed them too. "That's Mrs. Minelli and her daughter Sandra," she told me, sounding more relieved than I felt. "They live two blocks over." I'd never seen her before because I was only allowed to play on my own block. "Sandra will be in your class."

Mrs. Minelli and Sandra hadn't noticed us. Mrs. Minelli was busy retying the bows on Sandra's long blond pigtails. When we got to the corner, Mrs. Minelli looked up. "You must be Mrs. Cascone," she said to my mother, "and . . ." She looked at me.

"Gina," my mother told her. "And I'm Shirley."

"Beatrice Minelli," she introduced herself. "And this is Sandra," she presented her daughter, clearly expecting applause.

"Hi," I mumbled.

"Hello." Sandra smiled widely. "Aren't you excited? I am."

I shrugged. There was something wrong with one of us. I wasn't sure which one.

Meanwhile, my mother and Mrs. Minelli had established the fact that they had both gone to Catholic schools not far from one another. "Do you remember a Sister Agatha?" Mrs. Minelli asked. "She was transferred from your school to mine."

"Remember her." My mother shook her head, smiling. "How could I forget her? That one was something else." It was the same voice she used when she said that I was something else the day I made a spiderweb in the hallway with my bubble gum, sticking it and pulling it from wall to wall. I couldn't wait to hear about Sister Agatha.

"Yes," Mrs. Minelli answered, "she really is something special. I have her over to dinner quite frequently. Maybe you would like to come over sometime and see her again."

"That would be nice," my mother lied.

Sandra was still smiling. I couldn't go through with this. But it looked like it was too late; a bus turned onto the street about five blocks down.

"Looks like this is it." My mother patted my shoulder.

Not quite, I thought, devising a surprise attack. I knew that my mother was overly confident that this ordeal was over. I played on that. As the bus approached, I stood there sheepishly. When the bus was halfway down our block, I threw my lunch box at my mother and tore off toward home. I was fast, particularly when my adrenaline was running. While my mother was busy chasing me, the bus left without me. I got home before she did and locked her out of the house. But, having planned this on the spur of the moment and under acute pressure, I had neglected to take into account the fact that my father was still in the house. It was an impressive fight for freedom, but I was outnumbered. They took me alive. My father had to drive me to school, under ever-darkening skies. We had a terrible storm that day. I was sure it was an omen.

I sat in the car, watching my father out of the corner of my eye. Though his cheeks were throbbing the way they always did before a verbal explosion, his voice was calm. "Don't you want to go to school?"

Brilliant deduction. But then he is a lawyer, I told myself. You can't get anything past him. "No, I don't want to go to school," I pouted. I was furious that it had taken him this long to catch on to that fact. However, it had taken him and my mother both at least ten minutes to find me under the bed—the third time.

"Why not?"

I didn't answer.

"Is it the nuns?"

My stomach turned over inside me. I didn't want to be left alone with nuns. The only time I ever saw them was in church and they were always mumbling words that I didn't understand. How would I communicate with them?

My father had been watching for my reaction to the question and he must have seen my face pale at the mention of nuns. "Why are you afraid of the nuns?"

"I don't understand them."

Looking back, I don't think my father realized that I was worried about a language barrier. He thought my statement was more profound. After all, he didn't understand nuns either. "Ah, well," he hesitated, "there's nothing to be afraid of. Really, nothing at all. You'll see. Have I ever lied to you before?"

He'd told me it wouldn't be so bad having my tonsils out. And he'd promised that I'd just love fried peppers. But I was in no mood to listen to a speech on his integrity so I shook my head no.

We drove through the huge wrought-iron gates onto the expansive grounds of Saint Lucy's. I wondered if they closed those gates once all the kids were inside. We came to a stop in front of an enormous building. Farther down the path was another large white building and beyond that, the palatial-looking stone convent.

"You want me to park the car and come with you?" my father offered.

I shook my head no.

"You'll be all right?"

I nodded, reaching for the door handle.

"Don't I get a kiss?"

I leaned over and gave him an indifferent peck on the cheek.

He accepted my lack of affection and reached around me to unlock my door. He really overestimated me. I did a lot to keep from going to school, but I wouldn't have jumped out of a moving vehicle. He flung open the door and I slid out and slammed it shut behind me.

I didn't watch him drive away. I was absorbed in the scene that confronted me, of which I'd become a part. Uniformity. Tall kids, short kids, fat kids, skinny kids, all upholstered identically. I looked down at myself, then back up at the group milling around in front of me like zombies. I'd hated that uniform the first time I saw it, but now that I'd gotten the full effect of dozens of them before my eyes, I learned to loathe it.

Uniforms put a damper on summer. They had to be ordered in July. And the way kids grow, we all needed new ones every year. So every July I had to relinquish the sheer joy and abandon of summertime to be dragged to the store for an afternoon. Of course I wasn't alone in this. Kids from Catholic schools all over the city endured it. We never looked at each other while in the store. There was an unspoken ethic among us that we maintain our strength and dignity by not sharing our suffering. Whenever I looked around the store, I was sure I saw a number of unattended adults hanging around the uniform department. I knew why they were there—to catch the free show. Some of the most expressive faces in the world can be seen in the uniform department of clothing stores. The dressing room door would open and out shuffled the condemned child dressed in the drab gray and maroon, or gray and blue, or gray and green plaid. The scene that ensued was always the same.

"Mom," I would call in a whisper, not wanting to draw any attention to myself or come too far out into the store where other people might see me.

My mother never responded, she was always too busy collecting the necessary accessories: five white blouses; five pairs of gray socks; two gray sweaters; two bow ties; one beanie, hold the copter.

My eyes rolled back into my head, my hand slapped my cheek Jack Benny–like. "Mom," I called again in a sharp whisper. Mom continued about her business, oblivious to her mortified child. "Mo-ther," I hissed, finally capturing her attention.

"Oh, good." She smiled. She knew she was walking on eggshells. "Come here. Let me see how it fits."

My upper lip curled up like a vicious dog. "You come here," I warned.

She tried to humor me. She came over, kneeled down, slipped her fingers into the waistband to make sure there was enough room, tugged on it to straighten it out.

"What does it matter if it fits?" I growled. "I look like a jerk anyway."

"Now it's not that bad," Mom consoled.

My face said otherwise.

"Look." Mom dragged me over to the three-way mirror—a big mistake. "It looks kind of cute."

"You really think so, Mom?" I asked, wide-eyed.

Mom was relieved. She thought she was making headway. All she had to do was keep a straight face while she lied. "Sure."

"Good." I scowled. "We'll buy it for you. Because I'm not wearing it!"

Feeling a twinge of guilt for insulting my intelligence by lying, Mom nonetheless resorted to plan B. "You know, you should just be happy that you don't have to wear the kind of uniforms I did when I was in school," she reprimanded.

"I'd just be happy if I could go to public school like a normal person." Pauli popped into my mind, and I realized that I was grasping at straws.

"Don't start. Your father and I want to give you a better education. We want you to be someplace where you won't get lost in the crowd."

"That would be easier in prison. The uniforms are nicer there too. And I'll bet the food is better. And if you don't want to eat it, nobody's going to give you a lecture on the people who are starving in China."

Mom was laughing by now. She remembered. She knew how many times I'd heard her talking to her friends about their school experiences and fondly referring to the school as "the prison camp."

It didn't take me long to understand how accurate that image was. I often thought about war and prison movies where they put the hero in solitary confinement and you see him sitting there bouncing a ball off the wall, doing push-ups, pacing the cell. He does all these things in an effort to hang on to his ever slipping sanity in the face of constant denial and betrayal of human needs. The scene is an impressive testament to the durability of the human spirit. The classroom scene was comparable; a room full of children sitting in straight rows for hours on end, moving only as commanded; no ball, no push-ups, no talking, even to yourself.

The prisoners in the movies communicated by tapping on the cell walls. We had a system too—faces. I was surprised how eloquent a face can be. Of course, like the prisoners, we could communicate only along our own row. Turning around or making any gestures was just too risky. We couldn't even use cliché faces. For instance, you'd never stick out your tongue. If Sister happened to be using her rear-view vision while she was writing on the board and saw somebody stick out his tongue, she'd know what was going on. Our way, the most she could think was that we were sick, or better yet, that she was breaking us.

There were, however, hardships that even communication would not assuage, suffering that could not be alleviated. There was no way I was going to raise my hand and ask the person who gave the third degree about going to the bathroom: "Sister, may I please get up and walk around for a while because my behind is asleep?" Instead, I'd sit there saying to myself, "O God, no. This is it; the beginning of the end. No, the end of the end. How can I joke at a time like this? My body is beginning to atrophy." My mother told me that my brain would do that if I watched too much television. I won't be able to get in line for lunch. Then I'll starve to death in this godforsaken place. Good! Then I'll be out of my misery and my parents will finally believe me and be sorry that they did this to me. But the lunch bell rang and I slid out of my seat ever so gently to deter the onset of pins and needles. My brow was knit, my teeth clenched as I lifted myself out of the seat. The other kids knew what was wrong. It was a common malady. My legs buckled for a second, but I managed to get to the back of the room—last in line.

I never knew why we all rushed to get to the front of the line for lunch anyway. It was no reprieve; not even the lesser of two evils. The food was no worse than any other cafeteria really; just the standard, green-rimmed pork roll, the bottomless pit of mashed potato flakes, the watered soup, and stale bread and cakes. And every day we all stood and asked God to bless it. I'll tell you, for someone who could change water into wine and five loaves and a couple of fish into a repast for a multitude, the results we got were somewhat disappointing. The pork roll stayed green and tasted it as well.

And, as if we didn't have enough trouble getting this down, one of the nuns always had some grievance that she felt needed airing. Their favorite lunchtime dissertation was "What clogged the toilet?" This one came around once a month. The funny thing was that we were never exactly told what had clogged the toilet. No, of course not; it would have been far too easy that way. We had to sit there and "imagine," as we were commanded, how mortified Sister was when the plumber showed her what had caused the problem. How certain articles of feminine protection are not flushable. The way she described the condition of the bathroom, you would think that she had witnessed the scene of the Saint Valentine's Day Massacre. She pointed out the trauma that one of the younger children would have suffered had one by chance gone into that appalling bathroom. During one of these lectures, my classmate Dianne Luca leaned over and whispered to me "watch this." She punctuated Sister's point by throwing up right on the table. Actually she only spit out her mashed potatoes. She winked at me. Dianne and I would get along just fine.

Once, years later, Sister felt that she wasn't having the desired impact on us. She made us all line up right in the middle of lunch and file through the bathroom to see it for ourselves. Now, a toilet whose water level has run amok is a particularly unimpressive sight. After experiencing it, you can hardly expect to eat with the gusto you would if you had been looking over, say, the pastry cart. And let's not forget that we came back to the green pork roll, which I would gladly have flushed except that it would have clogged the toilet.

That day I'd really had it. I got up with my tray, making sure the path to the garbage can was clear of nuns. As I dumped the tray, I heaved a sigh of relief, then spun on my heels to return to my seat. But who was standing behind me but Sister Michael— hardly the archangel. Sister Michael was a lot like Zorro; always appearing out of nowhere, without a sound, ready to do battle. She was all dressed in black, and if she didn't have the mask, she did have a better mustache. "Young lady," she said, "do you know that there are people starving in China, people who would be grateful for the food you waste?"

An alarm went off in my head. "Enough. I'm not going to take any more. Let them expel me. Let my parents do anything they want to do to me. After this, anything is better." I looked right through Sister's glasses into her eyes. "Gee whiz, Sister," I answered her, "I thought of that myself and I was going to mail them my lunch. But then I figured that those poor people have suffered enough." She walked away as though she hadn't heard me. She must have known I was pushing for expulsion.

I returned to my seat to wait for the after-lunch, thank-you-for-this-great-meal-God prayer. Then we lined up to go out to the exercise yard. That was where we learned to play like "nice" children. Every class had a patrol girl, whose duty it was to keep order and avert riots. An effective way of doing this was to see that the entire class was involved in one game. Never hide and seek; always things like jump rope, where once again you found yourself standing in line forever. When Catholic kids grow up, you will find that they are particularly good standers-in-line. They'll stand on line in supermarkets until their frozen fish is swimming again, without one word of complaint.

We went through rigorous training learning not to complain. After all, Jesus was crowned with thorns, scourged at the pillar, forced to carry the cross to Calvary, and crucified. And all He had to say about this was, "Forgive them, Father, for they know not what they do." That made us feel a little guilty complaining about the discomforts we had to endure, like not being excused to go to the bathroom until we were certifiably jaundiced. The infuriating part was that we couldn't even take Jesus' attitude—because according to the nuns, nuns were not in need of forgiveness. Anything they did to us was only to make us better Catholics. Like the Lord, nuns work in mysterious ways.

Chapter 2

~

Creatures of Habit

SHE IS a myriad of wonders; a complete enigma. She is elusive and she means to be. The only thing of which I could be certain was that Sister was a "she." Of course, the only way I knew that was because that was how people referred to her. Establishing the fact that Sister was a "she" was little help though. I was a "she" and she was *nothing* like me. She wasn't anything like my mother, or my aunts, or the other women I knew. She wasn't even like my grandmother.

But whatever Sister was, she was more consistent than anyone I'd ever known. Day after day, her expression was unchanged, her behavior was unchanged, her clothes were unchanged! That same black drape every day that revealed only hands, a face, and occasionally, when she walked, a black shoe that poked out from underneath. There was no visible body. For all we knew, she could have been stuffed with straw or sawdust. No one had ever seen any one of the nuns perform any human function. We never saw them eat or take a drink of water, and certainly the only reason they ever went into a bathroom was to monitor us. By unspoken law, it was clear that we were not allowed to touch them. Was that because we might knock out their already loose stuffing?

Countless hours of precious recess time were given to speculation about the nuns. Finally, one rainy day, any theory that we may have had about the true nature of the nuns was destroyed. It was so windy that my umbrella got turned inside out; almost the best thing that happened to me that day.

When Sister Constance opened the door to the cafeteria so that we could get off the bus and run right inside, the wind blew her habit up and revealed a leg. We gaped. "Hurry, children," she commanded, oblivious to our astonishment. I couldn't believe what I'd seen. It was unmistakably a leg. We filed into the cafeteria and took seats around the long, formica-covered tables. It was one of the few times I was grateful for the mandatory silence. I couldn't be bothered with small talk. My mind was preoccupied. If there were legs under that habit, there had to be more and I wanted to know about it.

I sat there in the prescribed position, hands folded on the table, back straight, watching Sister Constance move up and down the aisles between the tables on patrol. When she passed me, I didn't lower my eyes as the others—and I usually—did. I stared right up at her. Though she didn't look back, I knew she saw me, possibly out of the eyes in the back of her head. They told us they had them. It was so that we wouldn't feel safe even when they had their backs to us. It worked.

After Sister Constance passed I saw the answer to all my

questions sitting right across from me. Roseanne. Roseanne lived in the convent. She was a boarder. There were several of them, but Roseanne was the only one in our class. I was sure she knew more about the nuns than I did. And even if she didn't, with a little effort she could probably find out. I started immediately on my campaign to get information. I bent over backward to be nice to her, plied her with homemade lunches, even stayed after school to play with her. Then I found out that she didn't know any more about the nuns than I did because they had completely separate living quarters. It didn't matter, though, because by then Roseanne and I were really friends.

Just about the time I'd given up hope of ever getting any kind of information, Roseanne rushed to the playground one morning, laughing and babbling nonsensically about some fashion show. Since she was sort of a scatterbrain—I could hardly blame her for it, considering the conditions under which she was forced to live—it took a while for me to get a coherent story out of her. The night before, the older girls had sneaked into the nuns' rooms. The girls knew they were safe for about an hour. It was Saint Lucy Filippini's feast day and all the nuns, who were of the Filippini order, were at mass at the same time and certainly not one of them would dare walk out. They found that the nuns' rooms, which are called cells, were just that: a closet, a dresser, one window, holy pictures and a crucifix on the wall, and a bed made so tightly you could bounce a quarter off it. Nothing was really very interesting, she told me, except the underwear, which the girls who had the courage to go into the rooms paraded around the halls. "They looked like my grandmother's," Roseanne laughed, "no, more like my grandfather's. And the bras, you could use them for hammocks."

Well that was it. They were women. To my way of thinking, they behaved very strangely and dressed even more strangely. For instance, my mind shot back to that fateful day when I saw

Sister Constance's leg. Nuns wore black stockings. Now that in itself may not be so strange. But my mother wore black stockings occasionally, when she was dressed up and had makeup on and her hair done, and my father couldn't keep his hands off her and kept telling her how great she looked. I got the distinct impression that the black stockings, for some reason, evoked this sort of behavior from men. But the nuns wore black stockings and they didn't have men. As a matter of fact, they were very clear on the subject of men. Men were like money—not having any was indicative of spiritual strength. A reasonable amount was a necessity for the average person and though it demonstrated a preoccupation with the pleasures of the world, it was entirely forgivable. An abundance increases the probability of the occasion of sin. So money was not the root of *all* evil; men made a fair contribution. And men have an edge on money because they are not, with any luck at all, inanimate objects. When you sin with money, you go to hell alone. But when you sin with a man, you take someone with you. And it is easier to resist money because it cannot pursue you.

However, the nuns saw to it that we took the proper precautions to ensure that men wouldn't pursue us. From the age of six, we were kneeling on the floor to make sure our skirts were long enough at least to touch. Even the high school girls were not allowed to wear makeup, nylons, or high heels. We were never allowed to cross our legs. This was something I didn't understand, particularly as I got older and it seemed to me that that should be exactly what they would want us to do. But the nuns insisted that crossed legs were legs that commanded attention and apparently legs are something that induce men to sin. Actually, the nuns made it quite clear to us that once you catch a man's eye, you've got him sinning. They can't help it; it's just the way they are. And once that starts, it's just a matter of time before they have you sinning right along with them. I understood this better than the nuns knew. You see, I'd caught my parents sinning. And God was mad all right. He stuck them with my first sister because of it. Frankly, at that stage in my life, I found sin disgusting and I didn't expect to understand its attraction for years to come. The nuns seemed to know this and were not so concerned with the purity of my soul in this matter as with protecting the souls of the men with whom I would come in contact. Now I knew I was cute, but I was really impressed that the nuns were worried about me being a siren at six. I figured that at this rate, by the time I was their age, even a habit wouldn't be deterrent enough.

Not that I ever, even for a second, considered being a nun. I looked terrible in black. And I asked far too many questions to be a nun. I rather enjoyed exercising the freedom of choice that they told us God gave us. Arbitrary obedience is not one of my strong points.

But none of this was relevant anyway. Call it "sour grapes" because I didn't get "the calling," that magical marriage proposal from God. Or worse yet, maybe I had and wasn't paying attention. I worried about it endlessly and the nuns were not the least bit reassuring. They were very secretive about "the calling," only discussing it with girls like Sandra Minelli who claimed she'd gotten it. Sandra was very smug about the whole thing and wouldn't tell *how* she'd gotten it. Did this "calling" come by phone, telegram, voices in the night? I prayed to God every night not to call on me. I didn't want to be a nun. But how do you say no to God? I knew I wanted to be married someday; but, frail creature that I am, I wanted a more tangible husband and a less solemn wedding ring. I found my mother's diamond solitaire much more appealing than the crucifix the nuns had wrapped around their fingers.

If I could have seen things more clearly, it would have been as obvious to me as it was to the nuns that there was no chance of God's calling me. I was far too unworthy. My priorities were all wrong. For instance, a nun was married to God. Who could ask for a better husband? He's got great job security, respectability, power, fame. Definitely someone you wouldn't be afraid to tell your mother about. Maybe my sights weren't high enough. I was looking for someone who would be home in the evening to talk to me, work with me, have fun with me, maybe even sin with me. I also wanted to be his only wife. Why, if God wanted to be a Mormon, were all his wives Catholic?

Apparently this double standard bothered some of them as well, since I knew a few who shed their habit to marry someone else. I supposed that they had to divorce God first. Because my father was a lawyer, I heard about divorce even when it was taboo. I wondered about the litigation involved in divorcing God. Seemed to me you could get Him on any number of counts: desertion, alienation of affections, polygamy. Personally, I would have opted for mental cruelty: forcing me to live in a harem, a dull one at that; only one dress to my name, the same ugly thing everyone else wore; having to get down on my knees whenever I addressed Him.

Still, I didn't think I should judge a guy by what goes on between him and his wife. I didn't care what the nuns said about Him, or how stern they tried to make Him appear, God seemed all right to me. I had no problem communicating with Him. I could talk to Him anytime, anywhere, in my own words. He never complained or insisted I do otherwise. I was certain that our relationship would be just fine as long as I didn't have to marry Him.

Chapter 3

~

Don't Drink
the Holy Water

WHETHER OR not you marry God, He wants to see you every week at His house on Sunday. These visits were traumatic for my parents because I embarrassed them so badly. Not because I was always standing when everyone else was kneeling. I was short enough to get away with it. Or because I walked on the kneelers even when my shoes were wet and muddy. Kids will do that. Even the fact that I treated mass like a matinee, munching on the penny candy that I had loaded my coat pockets with, didn't bother them. They figured that kept me quiet. My tap dancing in the aisles because I enjoyed hearing the mighty echo of my little feet was a bit more unnerving to them. They handled it well though, lifting me into the pew with the smile that showed everyone else what patient parents they were, but saying to me, "One more time and you'll never dance again." Even the time I spent the entire hour carefully picking the flowers off the hat of the woman in front of us, my mother kept a lid on it. The woman left church not knowing that she was wearing a plain straw hat—and my mother left with a pocketful of flowers. It took bigger things really to embarrass my parents. Bigger things, like the time I responded to the altar bell like one of Pavlov's dogs, grabbing a quarter out of the collection plate and running toward the sound screaming, "the Good Humor man." The one for which they've never forgiven me, though, was the day I decided to participate in the mass. After the choir finished the "Ave Maria" and the church was silent, I began my own little musical tribute to the man I admired most in this world—worshipped even—Paladin. The theme song to "Have Gun, Will Travel" resounded throughout the church. My voice carried impressively. My parents carried me out of the church.

Much as I tried, I just couldn't control myself. Magical things happened to me when I walked into a church; which was, as I understood it, the whole point. They told us that God and the angels were in there. To someone who had imaginary playmates, that wasn't beyond the realm of possibility. I took the phrase "choir of angels" quite literally, thinking that the voices I heard rising in songs of praise were the angels themselves. I was crushed when I found out that there was a choir and an organist in the balcony. Nonetheless, one does tend to rise to the level of those with whom one associates oneself. When you're playing with children, real or imaginary, you behave accordingly. When you're with God and the angels, you can't help but feel a sense of power. In church I felt powerful; more so since church is the only place where it seemed to me that adults didn't make the rules. I was completely awed by their behavior. It amazed me to see that adults were capable of such obedience and submission. I didn't think they had it in them.

But I could see why church would intimidate them. Now, I was well versed in language arts—quite fluent in English, Italian, and Pig Latin. I could even pick out a few words of Ubbi Dubbi. But what they were mumbling in church made no sense at all to me! And I could tell that most of the adults were lost as well. Week after week, I watched them trying to fake it, their lips all moving in different directions. I understood how that would unnerve adults; people so compulsive about being specific that they would spend half an hour debating exactly how many peas you had to eat before you got your pudding. And here they were, babbling away, with no idea what they were agreeing to.

Adults' defenses were made still weaker by the fact that many of them thought exercise was walking to the car or doing calisthenics. The routine in church of sit, stand, kneel, back straight, keep that butt off the pew, genuflect every time you change places completely wore them out. The only person I knew who could do it all correctly and keep those rosary beads moving at the same time was my grandmother. But it was tough to follow her lead because she was only a little bit taller than I was. You knew it was time to do something when you started to hear all the pews creaking, but you had to watch carefully to see if the crowd was going up or down. On top of all this, every now and then they rang a little bell. You weren't supposed to do anything in response to the bell. I figured they rang it to wake up those little old men who were always dozing.

I can't say that all this wasn't an interesting experience, and challenging, but my mind can only take so much boggling before I get fed up. Sharper minds than mine have been perplexed over this. Whether or not I participated, I still had to go to church. The problem that faced me was how to kill an hour sitting still.

You couldn't bring a bat and ball, deck of cards, or even your Dr. Seuss books. There I was, left with just me, my little white gloves, and little white purse with the rosaries and missal inside. There's not a whole lot you can do with gloves and a purse. And the only fun things you can do with rosaries are put them around your neck like a necklace or spin them on your finger like a small Hula-Hoop. Those are things that even I wouldn't try in church. That left the missal, which I couldn't read. The language looked worse on paper than it sounded. I found out that the language was Latin and that it was a "dead language." That certainly didn't surprise me. Nor did it surprise me that, like many of the saints, it went unburied by the Church.

I never did learn Latin. And I developed only a rudimentary knowledge of what was really going on. Desperate for something to do, I spent one entire mass trying to levitate a nun's bonnet to see what was underneath. It didn't work. But though I had a terrible headache, I was undaunted. Even Moses didn't part the Red Sea first time out, and he had help. What I had to do was start with small exercises for my mind. During the next mass I worked on memory. I closed my eyes.

Okay, where's the Blessed Mother?

Up front . . . left, I answered myself.

I opened my left eye for a quick peek. Right.

I did all the statues and all the stained glass windows without missing one. I even did some real trivia like, under which of the Blessed Mother's feet is the snake's head? The best game was during communion when everyone was walking to the front of the church. I would close my eyes and listen to the footsteps and try to guess who it was.

Shuffle. Clomp. Shuffle. Clomp.

That was Mrs. Roselli: about three hundred years old, black dress two sizes too big that hung almost to her ankles, where her stockings also hung. Her black pumps were also too big and just about fell off her feet every time she took a step. You could pick her out coming and going.

Pit-pat. Pit-pat.

Lena: as old as Mrs. Roselli, but wiry. She ran the corner candy store and during the summer when we went in to buy candy, she was always trying to feed us the tomatoes she grew in her backyard. If we ate the tomatoes and told her how great they were, she'd throw in a couple of extra pieces of candy. She was always the first and last stop on Halloween, which was when she cleaned out the counters.

Squeak. Squeak. Squeak.

Pauli Santini: sneaked into church with his sneakers on again. That would be good for later. We could watch his mother smack him on the head all the way home.

When there was a break in the footsteps, it was because there was a nun in line. They didn't make noise when they walked. That was so they could sneak up on kids. Picking out the nuns as they passed was a challenge. It took some work, but after a while I learned to do that too. It was dependent upon the kind of draft they caused and whether the smell was musty or mothballs.

That opened up another church game—sharpening the senses. Sometimes I loaded my purse with lots of small objects and, without looking inside, picked one up and tried to guess what it was by feeling it. The key to survival in church was creativity and discretion.

Once you got through communion, you had it made. After that even the adults were fidgety, getting their coats, purses, and kids ready to leave. They were also getting ready for the final battle before they got out of church—the votive candles, beloved of old ladies and young children. Church was the only place that, for a dime, kids could play with fire. That wasn't the point of the candles, of course. You were supposed to donate a dime to the

Church to light a candle and say a prayer for some special cause. It was sort of like tying string around God's finger; the burning candle was supposed to remind Him of the cause. And I guess the dime is to cover the cost of materials. Anyway, the candle stays lit until it burns itself out or until some bratty kid blows it out. Some kids used to blow blatantly as they walked past, knocking out a whole row of candles. I only blew out my own candle, the one I'd just paid for. I did it by praying extra whispery. That way, I was entitled to take the taper and light it all over again. It was all too rare that anyone under sixty got anywhere near the votive candles. There was only enough space for two on the kneelers in front of them and behind those two was a line a mile long. My mother used to rush me past, saying, "Next time you can light one. Besides, we want to get to the bakery before the crowd, don't we?" The promise of doughnuts was what got me into and out of church on Sunday mornings.

There was one last fascination before we got out the door. It was the holy water font, where everyone stopped to bless themselves. I used to have to reach up to dip my fingers in. It was wet and cold. And every week I strained on tiptoes to look inside the bowl. It was clear liquid and looked exactly like what came out of our tap at home, the same stuff that I drank and, under protest, bathed in. But it wasn't the same. At home it was just regular all-purpose water. This was HOLY water. I never knew where it came from or how it got holy, but I was sure it was powerful stuff. They throw it on babies to change them into Catholics. I've seen them do it. Oh, sure, the kid still screams; but he'll never dance naked around a fire and offer up a human sacrifice. And this is just the generic holy water. They have something even more powerful. As a matter of fact, something endorsed by the Blessed Mother herself—Lourdes water. Not only can that change somebody into a Catholic, it can also cure diseases. The AMA didn't worry about it too much, though. In order to be cured, you had to go to Lourdes. By the time you bought a plane ticket to France and paid for a hotel and food, it was cheaper to go to a doctor. And I found out later that there was another catch to the Lourdes water cure. You were only cured if it was God's will. I figured that God's will could find me just as easily at home.

Nonetheless, I could not disregard the stories of the miraculous powers of holy water. While the other kids were busy flicking it at one another, I dipped my fingertips in and reverently made the sign of the cross on myself. Some kids even scooped some water out in the palm of their hand and licked it! I have to admit, I wondered what would happen if I drank holy water. Would it change me? It certainly never changed Pauli and he drank it every week. But maybe with his innards coated with holy water he was immune to disease. At least he never seemed to get sick. Still, I decided not to risk it. You don't know who's been dipping their hands into that holy water or what effect it will have if you drink it. One of the teenage girls on my block got a baby from swimming in the public pool and pool water isn't nearly as potent as holy water. I decided to leave the drinking to Pauli. It couldn't possibly hurt him.

Apparently the priest got just as worried about this drinking problem as I was. Instead of leaving a bowlful of water, he put a wet sponge in the font. He must have figured that no one would suck on a sponge. He underestimated Pauli.

Chapter 4

❦

Bless Me, Father,
for I Am Sinning

G OING TO church became increasingly important during
my second grade year. Until now, I had only attended
church as an observer. Soon, I would be indoctrinated as an
active participant. According to the rules of the Church, I had
come of age. Seven. The age of reason. I wasn't allowed to cross
the street yet—but I was made to understand that now I was
totally accountable for my sins. What sins? At seven you can't
even understand most of the commandments, much less break
any of them. No dogmatic problem! There was the Catholic door
prize, Original Sin. Since you hadn't time or the opportunity to
accumulate any of your own, they gave you a starter sin—

Original. Actually I think it was only a cheap reproduction and it was sort of hard to feel genuine guilt over it. But with a little time and conditioning, you began to feel as though you were the original perpetrator—a real trick, since at seven you didn't even know what Original Sin was. As a matter of fact I'm not too clear on it to this day.

That apple story is terrible PR for God. It makes Him look really petty; I mean, one lousy apple. He had a whole treeful. If a friend broke one of my toys, my mother would say, "Now come on, don't be angry, you've got a whole roomful of toys." You mean to tell me that I was supposed to be more forgiving than God? And the extent of my retaliation would have been, at most, a smack or refusing to play with him for the rest of the day. I certainly wouldn't have exiled him and cursed his progeny for all time.

If you really think about it, it looks as though God had premeditated the whole thing. Take any normal, healthy human being and tell him he's got the run of the place, he can do anything he wants to do except touch that tree over there in the corner. Oh, he might make it through the first day without thinking about the tree. But the second day that tree will be creeping into his thoughts constantly. Then he won't be able to get it out of his mind. Soon he'll be obsessed with the tree. When he feels himself coming apart at the seams, when he just can't take it anymore, he's going to go and jump on that tree. And God's sitting there right behind the tree ready to get him for it. Talk about sadism. It's like teasing a dog with a piece of meat and then punishing the poor animal when he finally gets it.

Aha! But herein hangs the tail. The whole point is that God gave us something that He didn't give to the animals, a free will. He was acutely disappointed that after all His hard work, Adam and Eve abused the gift. He gave them everything and asked in return obedience of one small rule. See, if you look at it from

God's point of view, not only do you begin to understand God's wrath, but you'd rather like the opportunity to get a shot at them yourself. After all, it's their fault that we're here struggling to survive, instead of lounging around the Garden of Eden.

The whole Adam and Eve story is a tremendous embarrassment to the human race. Not only do we have Adam and Eve, the original sinners, but they have two kids, Cain and Abel. Cain kills Abel, his own brother. The only decent member of the family gets iced. This is from whence we come? You can't help but feel ashamed to be human. Now you've got it—Original Sin. You still can't quite put your finger on it, but you're feeling miserable and that's enough. You can't wait to get into that confessional and purge your soul of this smirch. We didn't even mind coming in early from recess to learn confessional etiquette.

That spring while the other kids were outside playing jump rope, we were inside playing confession. First we had to make believe that Sister Michael was Father Joseph. That was a cinch; she did, after all, have a mustache and we all suspected that she was as bald as he was too. It would have been a lot more fun if we could have practiced with Father Joseph, which is exactly why the nuns did their best to keep us away from him. He was a real sucker for little girls. He used to call us "sweet souls," and put his hand on our heads and bless us like this: "May God bless you and keep you. And don't forget to say a prayer for me," and then he'd wink. He made us believe that God loved us like crazy. And that's why he was no good for teaching confession. To Father Joseph, we were sweet souls, not tarnished ones.

Sister Michael, on the other hand, was perfect for the job. It was her attitude that it was a sin for a kid even to be alive. And she made *you* sorry for it too. The idea must have been, if you could confess to Sister Michael, you could confess to any priest. In the nine years I spent in Catholic school, I never saw Sister Michael enjoy herself more than when we played confession.

The sight of so many penitent children must have warmed the cockles of her heart.

Making up sins is a lot tougher than committing them and not nearly as much fun. You really had to be careful to make up a good confession for Sister Michael; too few sins and she knew that you were going to lie in confession, too many and she was going to keep an eye on you for the rest of the year. You had to be careful about the kinds of sins you made up. "I ate meat on Friday," or "I missed mass on Sunday," were definitely out. You didn't even want her to know that such things entered your mind. That would have offered her the opening for an unendurable lecture. It was better to stick to sins that she herself had accused us of committing—like being disrespectful, disobedient, and inconsiderate. That was the format we all stuck to. Except Dianne Luca. I'd already done my confession and gotten my penance—say the rosary every day for a week—and was back in my seat when Dianne got to the front of the line.

She went up to the desk and knelt down next to Sister Michael. "Bless me, Sister, for I have sinned."

"Father," Sister corrected her.

"Oh, yeah, right. Anyway, this is my first confession."

"Dianne, I think you should do it again."

"Bless me, Father, for I have sinned. This is my first confession."

"That's better. Now, Father may say something to you or he may not. So just pause a minute and if he doesn't say anything, go ahead with your sins." Sister must have thought that we were either idiots or hard of hearing; she went over the same thing with every single kid.

"Okay. Well, I have graven idols, I committed murder, and I coveted my neighbor's wife."

The class broke up. Sister did not. "I do not," she announced, "and I am sure God does not," she name-dropped, "find this amusing. Young lady, your immortal soul is not something to joke about."

Dianne was just as annoyed as Sister was. "You told us that you didn't want to hear our real sins. Those were the ones I *didn't* commit."

"Not yet, anyway," Sister said under her breath. Dianne was voted by the nuns most likely to achieve notoriety before puberty. "Well, I think that's enough for today." She didn't even give Dianne penance, leaving us all to wonder how many prayers murder rates.

After two weeks of simulated confessions, we were ready for the real thing. While we stood in line in front of the confessional, we were supposed to be "examining our consciences," and working out what we would say to Father. But we'd spent the past two weeks doing that and I had my account of the errors of my ways down pat. I was getting bored. I was too far back in line even to try to hear what was going on inside the confessional. Besides, I knew that all Father was going to hear was a recital of infractions of the fourth commandment—Honor thy father and thy mother—pretty dull stuff. If I went into the priest business, I would have specialized in adult confessions. I was sure they had to be much more interesting. And to make it even more fun, you could play match the sins to the parishioners. I would have just loved to find out that all those sodality ladies, who prayed at everyone's funeral, were spending their free time creating a demand for their services. But I was sure that their confessions went more like: "Bless me, Father, for I have sinned. Last Friday I spent the whole day working funerals and I forgot to cook dinner for my family. You see, by the time I got home I was so tired that I had forgotten what day it was. I pulled some leftover meat loaf out of the refrigerator and warmed it up. We were halfway through dinner before I realized that I had caused my entire family to participate in this grievous sin. Of course the moment I realized, I stopped them all, which is the source of more guilt, Father. I hadn't gone food shopping and there was nothing else in the house for dinner. Because of me, my family went hungry."

Father forgives her sins and for penance has her work next Friday's funeral circuit and then come home and have a fish fry for the whole neighborhood.

As I thought about it, I decided that adults were probably as careful as we were not to make their confessions too colorful. Then it dawned on me that nuns went to confession too. For what? All they ever did was pray. The only commandment they even came close to breaking was the fifth. But to my knowledge, none of them had ever succeeded in murdering a kid, and close isn't enough. Maybe they had to make up sins like we did. You couldn't be a good Catholic, after all, unless you had something about which to feel guilty and beg God's forgiveness, even if it was lying to the priest in confession because you didn't have any real sins. I was grateful that I had some real sins at least for this first confession.

When my turn came, I stepped into the little closet and knelt down on the wooden kneeler. While I waited for Father Joseph to slide open his window, I thanked God that I wasn't claustrophobic or afraid of the dark. He slid open the panel and before I had a chance to go into the "Bless me, Father" routine, he said, "Hello, sweet soul. So this is your first confession."

"Yes, Father."

"And there are some things that you want to tell God that you're sorry for having done."

"Yes, Father."

"Well, why don't you go ahead, then."

I recounted my violations of the fourth, still feeling that my parents had actually instigated some of those indiscretions.

"I'm sure you didn't really mean to do those things."

"No, Father." He understood how tough it is to deal with parents sometimes.

"And you're going to try not to do them again."

"Yes, Father."

"Well, we all make mistakes. God understands that."

That's not the way Sister tells it. He went into his forgiveness prayers, in Latin of course. Since we'd rehearsed, I knew it was time for me to ignore him and say my Act of Contrition. We finished.

"Why don't you say two Hail Marys and one Our Father just to let God know that you're thinking about Him. And . . ."

I could tell by the inflection in his voice what he wanted me to say, so I said, "And don't forget to say a prayer for you."

He chuckled. "That's a good girl."

"Thank you, Father," I said as I stood up.

"God bless you, sweet soul." He slid down the panel.

So that was it—the wrath of God. Sister Michael would have been disappointed in Him.

Chapter 5

Ashes and Sackcloth

GOD IS all knowing, all loving, and all forgiving. But then
He can afford to be. He is after all, God. However, even He
has His limits. You can only push Him so far and He's going to
fly off the handle like anybody else. Look at what He did to
Sodom and Gomorrah. And let's not forget Noah's ark. It could
happen again. The Bible says it will. The nuns assured us that
Armageddon would come. But it didn't have to be in our lifetime. We could impede it with repentance. It was only when we
stopped atoning for our own sins that God would be forced to
take matters into His own hands. So, as a favor to us all, the
Church took it upon itself to deal with crime and punishment.

We never got any of the juicy details about the sins. The nuns were extremely vague about what was going on in Sodom and Gomorrah that sent God into a tantrum. And it was one hell of a tantrum too. He annihilated both cities and all their inhabitants, except Lot and his family. But as they left, Lot's wife looked back, against strict orders from God. Because she disobeyed Him, He turned her into a pillar of salt. Now it seems to me that you just don't do that to a guy's wife, particularly on a first offense. But because He was in such a foul mood, He really let her have it for something He probably would have let pass normally.

I'll just bet, knowing what I do of God, that He isn't as proud of that Sodom and Gomorrah business as the nuns were. Actually they weren't really proud of it as much as they were terrified by it. Nuns tend to be much more afraid of God than most people. I can understand why they would be. God has warned us that we've already pushed our luck to the limit. Next time it's Armageddon and lights out for everybody. If we all run around sinning like crazy, we deserve Armageddon. But *we* will have had our fun. The nuns are going to get it too, though; and I am certain that they don't have any fun at all, at least not in the biblical sense. Nuns are perfectly willing to lay down their lives for any cause—except for someone else's cheap thrills. That's only fair. So it is easy to understand that they would go to any lengths to constrain us from sinning.

Scaring the wits out of children has been proven quite effective. We'd been told enough stories to know that we didn't want to leave punishment for our sins up to God. If the nuns were right, He lets things build until He's pushed to extremes. The nuns made it clear that we were much better off letting punishment for sins be doled out by the Church. Compared to global destruction, a hair shirt or even self-flagellation was a welcome alternative. But alas, gone were the good old days that Sister Michael longed for, when contrition was more physical. I always suspected that Sister Michael needed something physical in her life. A hair shirt would have worked wonders for her. But according to her rules, which she told us came right from the top, we were the ones in need of repentance.

The classic penance was to sit in the town square with ashes on your forehead, dressed in sackcloth. We saw the modernization of this ritual at least once a week. The penitent in this scene was usually Dianne Luca. Instead of sitting in the town square with ashes and sackcloth, she was sitting on the windowsill with a dunce cap on her head. If she'd earned this dishonor for amusing the class with stories of which "uncle" spent the previous night with her mother, she also had tape over her mouth. But if she was up there for perpetrating one of her notorious staple gun attacks on Sandra Minelli, she had milk cartons on her hands.

Roseanne's penance, though more private, was no less classic. Because Roseanne lived at the convent, the nuns used to help her get ready for school. She had very long hair, with which she needed help brushing. In dealing with children, Sister Michael had all the gentility and grace of a sumo wrestler. The way that nun brushed Roseanne's hair, the poor kid was scared to death that she was going to end up looking like Ben Franklin: bald on top, with tufts of shoulder-length hair dangling from the sides. Not to mention the physical pain it caused her. Roseanne had the best "horror movie" scream in school and she used it every morning. Of course that doesn't bother nuns. Eerie stuff is their specialty. What annoyed Sister about Roseanne's screaming was that it displayed, in her opinion, a lack of endurance of discomfort. A good Catholic should be able to smile through crucifixion; and here was a kid who couldn't stand to have her hair brushed. Sister just wouldn't have that. One morning she decided that it was time to remedy the problem. She went into Roseanne's room and emptied a cup of rice onto the linoleum floor. As Sister did this, Roseanne innocently asked, "What about all the people starving in China?" That bought her five extra minutes kneeling on the rice. For fifteen minutes she knelt silently on the rice. Then she got up and picked half of it out of her knees, cleaned up what was on the floor, and screamed like hell when Sister brushed her hair. Sister gave up with Roseanne.

My shortcoming, as Sister Michael saw it, was an acute lack of faith. I asked too many questions. So one day on the playground, Sister decided to initiate an exercise in blind faith. We all got into a circle and someone got into the middle, closed their eyes and fell back, trusting that someone else would catch them. When it came my turn to be in the middle, I made sure I was standing with my back to Sandra Minelli. She was the one who would have liked to have seen me fall and knock myself out more than anybody. But with Sister standing right next to her, I knew that if she couldn't catch me, she would at least throw herself onto the ground to break my fall. I fell and Sandra caught me and we both smiled at Sister. She was thrilled at the progress she was making with me.

Sister didn't have to give Sandra penance. Sandra took that responsibility herself. She would give up recess to go to the chapel and pray. She gave up candy. And, when she'd done something totally heinous, like forgetting to say her rosary the night before, she would spend the entire recess period kneeling on the play-ground. To me, her rapture and enjoyment of punishment seemed to defeat the purpose of repentance. But, once again, I must have been wrong because Sister encouraged her every step of the way. She told us stories about saints who would wear hair shirts under their clothes that would literally tear the flesh from their bodies. Or saints who would beat themselves with a cat-o'-nine-tails. Sandra's only question was where could she buy one. With a look of deep regret, Sister told her that you couldn't anymore.

I had a question too. "Why? Why did they do these things?"

"To remind themselves of the pain that sin causes God."

"So they hurt themselves on purpose?"

"Yes, they did."

My mother would kill me if she caught me acting nutty like that. I didn't say that to Sister, though.

Dianne Luca had something to contribute to this conversation. She raised her hand and waved it in the air for a while until Sister couldn't pretend that she was invisible anymore. "Yes, Dianne," Sister said, expecting the worst.

"One of my uncles is always trying to hurt himself on purpose. And you know what, Sister, it doesn't work. It didn't get him to heaven—they took him to the sanitorium."

"Lord have mercy." Sister leaned against her desk. No matter what Dianne said, that was how Sister answered.

"That's just the point, Sister," Dianne continued. "He didn't. I don't think God likes it when people hurt themselves," she said in earnest.

"Yes . . . well . . . I'm sure you're right, Dianne. And none of us here will do that." That put an end to the topic of painful penance for a while.

The day Dianne told everyone that Sister Constance was a truck driver before she became a nun, Sister Michael told us her only painless penance story.

It seems there was this guy who went to confession because he indulged in a little gossip about someone else. The priest told him to take a feather pillow to the highest bell tower in the city. When he got there, he should wait for a good, strong wind, tear open the pillow, and shake the feathers into the wind and watch them blow across the city. When the feathers were out of sight, he was to leave the tower and collect up all the feathers and then he would be forgiven. The man protested that this was impossible. The priest pointed out that his gossiping was equal to scattering the feathers. Collecting the feathers would be easier than finding and repairing the damage he had done to another man's reputation.

However many times Sister Michael may have told this story

in the presence of Father Joseph, he never seemed to catch on. All the nuns were disappointed in his lack of dramatic flair when it came to his meting out of penance.

They watched us go in and out of the confessional and kneel down for a couple of minutes to say our two Hail Marys and one Our Father and an extra prayer for Father Joseph. They never saw anyone picking up feathers or anything else around the grounds. They knew what kind of penance we were getting and they weren't happy about it. But confession was Father Joseph's department and there was nothing they could do about it. No matter what we did, penance was always the same. You could go in there and tell him that you had just burned down the convent and he'd tell you that God knew that you didn't mean to be bad and he'd give you two Hail Marys and one Our Father and "Don't forget to say a prayer for me."

Nobody ever forgot to say that prayer for him—though he was the last person in the world who needed prayers. He went out of his way to try not to inspire awe. The only time we saw him with his collar on was in church. Otherwise you could find him dressed in a plaid flannel shirt and Levi's, taking care of the hundreds of plants he had growing everywhere. His favorite were the pansies. He loved the faces they made almost as much as the ones we made. He always caught us doing that and he'd wink just to let us know.

Father Joseph believed that everyone was as well-intentioned as he was. I don't think he believed in sins, just mistakes, and those he expected. He never did or said anything to make us afraid of God or feel unworthy of His love. Confession with Father Joseph was not accepting punishment but responsibility, and I came away not fearing God's wrath, but wanting His approval. After confession I felt as though I understood the meaning of the mass and communion. Only one problem remained: how to get holy communion off the roof of your mouth.

Chapter 6

How to Get
Holy Communion
off the Roof of
Your Mouth

FIRST YOU lick it. Then you suck it. Then you give up and leave it alone, because you're not allowed to touch it with your fingers. So you spend the last few minutes of the mass praying that you don't choke. I was always worried about that—so worried that I decided to throw caution to the wind and ask Sister about it.

"Sister, you're not supposed to touch the Host, right?"

"That's right."

"Never?"

"Never."

"What if you're choking on it?"

"Not even then."

"But what if you die!?"

"Then you'll go straight to heaven."

Hardly a comforting thought. Luckily, I had my father's eye for loopholes. If I ever started to choke on a Host, I was going to stick my finger in there and save my life. Then I'd go to confession, say my two Hail Marys and one Our Father to have God forget all about it, and wind up alive, forgiven, and ready to go to heaven some other time.

With that problem solved, there was only one thing that bothered me about communion and that was that they told us it was the "body of Christ." I was a kid who had trouble eating meat after I found out it came from living creatures. The first time they told me that communion was the "body of Christ" and I had to eat it, I broke into a cold sweat. Even I didn't have the courage to ask if they at least cooked it first. But I'd seen Hosts up close. They were about the size of a half-dollar but thinner and white. They didn't look anything like any part of anybody's body. Still, I didn't trust it. The first time I received communion I just let it lay there on my tongue. Even without my help, it started melting in my mouth. It wasn't bad; kind of sweet actually. For a minute I wondered if it tasted that good because it was "the body of Christ."

But as I sat there licking it, trying to keep it from getting stuck to the roof of my mouth, I began to recognize the taste. Yes, it was definitely familiar. I had to think about it for a while before it came to me—flying saucers. That was it. Holy communion tasted just like flying saucers. Lena, who ran the corner candy store, sold them two for a penny. They even looked like communion wafers, except Lena's were two dome-shaped wafers stuck together with BBs in the middle. Once we all made the connection, Lena did a booming business with flying saucers. We'd all pool our money and go down to the store and buy as many flying saucers as we could. Then we would spend the next half hour splitting them in half and taking out the little candy BBs. That was the only reason we let Pauli play. We needed someone to eat all of those BBs. If we threw them away on the ground, Lena would come out and chase us away with her broom. Having Pauli there, we ran the risk of having Lena come out and chase us away with her broom anyway. But we knew how to control Pauli. All you had to do was smack him on the head when he started to get out of line.

Once we got the wafers apart and stacked them up, it was time to elect a priest. I never volunteered to be the priest. If you were the priest, you just stood there on the steps and gave out the communion. I liked eating them myself. So I forfeited the respectability of the position for baser rewards. Pauli always wanted to be the priest. He never got any votes, though. Nobody wanted to eat something after Pauli touched it. The one time we did give in and let him be the priest, he took off with the whole stack of wafers. We didn't bother to chase him. We really didn't want them back after they'd been in the same pocket as his frog. Sandra Minelli wouldn't play holy communion at all, even if she could be the priest. She told us that first of all she didn't want to be a priest, she wanted to be a nun. And secondly, impersonating a holy person was a sacrilege punishable by eternity in hell. Besides, she pointed out, it wasn't even realistic. Holy communion wafers were white. Flying saucer wafers were all different colors. Technicalities. You would think that someone whose mind was capable of believing that some little cookie was the body of Christ could make believe that a blue one was white. Sandra never played and we never cared.

Lena didn't mind when we played communion on her steps. It kept us quiet and she was sure it would encourage us to grow up to be diligent Catholics. Sometimes she'd even throw a few extra saucers in the bag, her contribution to the spiritual well-being of the world. There were days when we were in a financial pinch and couldn't afford Lena's. But that didn't mean we couldn't play communion. All we needed was a loaf of bread and a round cookie cutter. We would cut three circles out of each piece of bread. Again we needed Pauli. We couldn't let anybody's mother see a mutilated piece of bread in her garbage. We had to roll the leftovers into a ball. Pauli loved bread-balls almost as much as BBs. He took care of the evidence for us again. Once we'd cut out all the circles of bread, we had to pound them flat before we were ready to play.

All the time we played holy communion did not help alleviate the pressures I felt during the real thing. I hated sticking my tongue out in front of the priest. I never understood how he managed not to laugh. People look really stupid standing there with their tongues hanging out. Especially Mrs. Roselli: when she took communion, she looked like a frog catching a fly. It made me laugh every time, but Father kept a straight face. I prayed that I didn't look like Mrs. Roselli when I got communion. What bothered me more than the fear of looking stupid was when Father's fingers touched my tongue. He didn't react to it at all. Inside though, I knew he had to be cringing and dying to be able to go wash his hands. I was so embarrassed. Then I wondered how many other tongues he touched and what kind of germs he'd picked up along the way. It had to be much worse for him than it was for me. That was probably why he had to fortify himself with that glass of wine before he did it.

The only time we ever got wine in church was once on Holy Thursday. They decided to reenact the Last Supper, so we all got to partake in the body and blood of Christ—bread and wine, symbolically. After the priest put the wafer in your mouth, he gave you the chalice to take a sip of wine. It was emptied a few times along the way and he refilled it. When my turn came, it was full. I could get away with a healthy swig and it wouldn't make any difference. It would wash the wafer down without my having to worry about choking. I took the chalice and put it to my lips without a thought of all the other people who drank from that same cup. Even an unsophisticated palate could tell that this was not Chateauneuf du Pape. And I had a good mouthful too. Luckily, I had a talent for swallowing terrible things; I ate in the school cafeteria every day. With my mouth full of wine, I took a deep breath in, then let it out, swallowed quickly in one gulp, then immediately drew in as much fresh air as my lungs could hold. Done.

Pauli was next to me. As I got up from the kneeler, I watched him take the chalice. He drained it, smacked his lips, and handed it back to Father. Father turned calmly and went back to the altar to fill it. Priests almost never have to do the dirty work. That's why the church is always crawling with nuns—they keep law and order. They are the enforcers. There was a nun right behind Pauli. She saw what he'd done. As he got up, she smacked him on the head. Being smacked on the head was as natural to Pauli as breathing, so he never reacted to it. I always suspected that sooner or later all that smacking on his head would have the same effect on Pauli as kicking does on a television that's on the blink. It would either snap him into focus or put his lights out. Either way it would be an improvement. Now, a nun can't do anything as awesome as turn anyone into a pillar of salt, but they do have connections. When Pauli started to stumble a little on his way back to the pew, I figured that Sister had given him that magic smack. But when he started laughing more than usual in church, I realized that it wasn't because Sister hit him, but because the wine did.

We weren't allowed to eat for three hours before, and one hour after receiving communion. The only explanation I could come up with for this one was that the body of Christ does not mix well with doughnuts. So you just keep all the riffraff out of your stomach until He's through. I suppose you could eat something and no one would know, if you brushed your teeth real well. But when the body of Christ got down there and found out He wasn't alone, He might try to evacuate. And there was nothing in the whole world that I was more afraid of than throwing up.

When I was sick, I would fight that urge for hours—which wasn't easy because at the first inkling that I had an upset stomach, my mother would put a bucket next to me. It's very difficult to convince yourself that you're not going to throw up when you're lying there staring into a bucket. So rather than taking any chances of facing the bucket, I refrained from eating for the three hours before and one hour after communion.

And when our voices were not raised in praise of God, our stomachs let their protests be heard, which one little wafer did little to silence. I couldn't help thinking that if Jesus were there in the flesh, He'd turn those wafers into ham and eggs for all of us. He liked to see people enjoying life. He could afford to take that attitude; He was the son of God. He was entitled to look at the joy in what His Father had created. Jesus would always be with God but that was a privilege that the rest of us really had to work to receive.

The nuns never let us forget that. There was far too much to be done in this life than spend time living it. Where we are now is not a permanent arrangement. We're all headed somewhere else. People are dying to find out where. And that's exactly the way to do it.

Chapter 7

≈

All Things Considered,
I'd Rather Be in Limbo

WHERE DO you go after you die?
        My only experience with death at seven was the day
after the school carnival when I found the goldfish I won doing the
dead man's float. I knew he hadn't learned it at the Y. Something
was wrong. I called my mother. She explained to me that the fish
was dead. She relieved a surge of guilt by convincing me that it
wasn't because I'd beaned him with the Ping-Pong ball. Since I
hadn't had much time to cultivate a relationship with my fish, the
emotional impact of his passing was mild. My mother offered a
few effective words of comfort, then flushed him down the toilet.
That was it—my knowledge of death. Beyond that I was lost.

44

Thankfully, I knew I was already too big to flush, so I knew I wasn't going where the goldfish went. Where I *was* going was a mystery to me. Actually, I wasn't really interested. I'd only just gotten here and I wasn't sure enough about where I was to worry about where I was going.

The nuns, however, worried about where everybody was going. They were like God's travel agents, helping us all make our reservations well in advance. We had a choice of four possible destinations: heaven, hell, purgatory, and limbo. With heaven, you get a bliss-filled eternity with God. In hell, you spend all of eternity at the mercy of the sadistic Devil. Purgatory is a layover in hell, with heaven the ultimate destination. And limbo is just like heaven but without God's presence. In any case, the excursion begins at the pearly gates, where Saint Peter checks your reservations. I always thought that this was sort of a crummy job for the guy who established the Church of Rome.

The surest way to get right past Peter into heaven was to wear a scapular at all times. A scapular is about three feet of string with two cloth holy pictures attached to it. You wear it around your neck so that one picture hangs in front and the other hangs in back. It's something that the priest puts around your neck on your first communion to protect you through life and death. In addition, I had a gold horn around my neck to protect me from the *mal'occhio* evil eye; a gold cross to protect me from accidents; and, if my grandmother had her way, I would have had a sack of garlic to protect me from sickness. She and my father used to fight about it. He spent most of his childhood with garlic around his neck and he knew from firsthand experience that if I wore garlic around my neck, it would indeed keep germs away from me; germs and all other living things, except Pauli. I went without the protection of garlic. What I really needed was a padded collar to protect me from strangulation.

If you die with your scapular on, you go straight to heaven, no questions asked. Your chances of dying are greatly increased with your scapular on, particularly when you're sleeping. Every time you roll over, that string winds itself around your neck. I woke up every morning with marks all over my neck and every morning my mother tried to get the scapular away from me. I refused to give up my ticket to heaven. Then one night, my mother came up with the brilliant idea of pinning the scapular to my nightgown so that it couldn't wrap around my neck. She went to bed secure that I would still be there and not in heaven in the morning. But during the night, the safety pin opened and stabbed me in the back. My mother did not appreciate being awakened from a sound sleep by a bloodcurdling scream. That was the end of the scapular.

My mother assured me that there were better ways of getting to heaven. After all, it wasn't Sister Michael who guarded the pearly gates; it was Saint Peter. I was sure it took a lot more than a scapular to impress him. If a scapular is all it takes to get into heaven, why did God bother to write all those commandments? And why didn't Jesus just spend his time on Earth passing out scapulars? He could have saved himself all that aggravation and avoided trouble with the Romans.

I stopped worrying about not wearing a scapular and started looking into other ways to beat the system. If you die right after you go to confession and do your penance you get straight into heaven. That's why drivers have to be particularly careful in front of churches. There are a lot of Catholics who aren't worried about being run over. The nuns told them the same thing when they were kids, and some people are more anxious than others to get there.

All in all, getting directly into heaven is dependent upon dying at an opportune moment: after confession, after communion, after baptism, after the last rites, or with your scapular on. Most people don't go at opportune moments and God can get around the scapular business by catching you in the shower. If that happens, chances are that you will end up in purgatory. Purgatory is for people who try to be good but can't quite overcome being human. It's a stint in hell to put the fear of God in you. Sister insisted that in order to get to heaven, we had to fear God. I couldn't understand why I would want to go to heaven to be with God if I was afraid of Him. I wasn't afraid of God. I was afraid of the Devil and that was why I didn't want to go to hell. I was also afraid of Sister and that was why I didn't want to go to school. But there I was, doing time with Sister; and I figured that I'd end up doing time with the Devil too. Hopefully that would only be in purgatory, where I had hope of getting out.

Getting from purgatory to heaven was even more tricky than getting directly into heaven. Once you land in purgatory, there is nothing you can do to help yourself get out. Getting out quickly is entirely dependent upon the good graces of others. Every prayer offered up for your soul shortens that sentence, but those prayers have to come from Earth. This is something to consider when drawing up a will. Leave everything to people who pray a lot and hope for the best. In the meantime, you have to sit tight and wait for heaven the same way we waited every day for the three o'clock bell. The waiting is grueling and torturous, but it does have an end.

On the other hand, hell, like heaven, is eternal. And, like heaven, getting there depends heavily upon your checkout timing. If you happen to die after you have eaten meat on Friday and before you get to confession and you don't have your scapular on, you should pack your warm-weather clothes and bring along some salt tablets. Nobody could explain why eating meat on Friday was so bad. Nowhere in the commandments does it say, "Thou shalt not eat meat on Friday." I don't know what practical joker slipped that rule in in the first place. But the Church finally caught on and rescinded it. What happened to all the people who ate meat on Friday before the rule was declared null and void? Did they really go to hell? And once the rule was changed, did God grant them a blanket pardon? The whole situation has to be very embarrassing to God. How do you apologize to someone for sending them to hell for no good reason?

The truth is that I couldn't believe that God sent anybody to hell. Sister could threaten all she wanted; I wasn't buying any of it. I figured that keeping me at her mercy was as punitive as God would get. I ruled out hell as a possibility. By virtue of baptism, limbo wasn't a possibility, either. Limbo was where pagans went; all pagans—good, bad, or mediocre. It was just like heaven except that God wasn't there. But that wouldn't matter to a pagan because he wouldn't know Him anyway. Being a pagan sounded like a pretty good deal. You could indulge in extremely antisocial behavior, eat anything you wanted to whenever you wanted to, not have to go to church, worry about cleanliness, or even wear clothes; and still end up in a great place. And all this because somebody didn't throw water on you. When Sister would speculate on how much time I would be spending in purgatory for my myriad of sins, I would pray, "Dear God, if I can't make heaven, please just send me to limbo. It's not my fault they got me with that water. I was a defenseless baby. Sure I'll miss you in limbo. But it will be a lot nicer than missing you in purgatory, and infinitely better than hell. And in limbo it will be much easier to cling to fond memories of you."

I thought a lot about getting into heaven and what it would be like. If I had to go, it was my first choice. On warm days, I would lay in the grass and stare up at the sky. I was sure that heaven was just the other side of the clouds. I would watch planes disappear into the clouds and wonder if they caught a glimpse of heaven. And as I lay there staring up at the bottom of the clouds, I was positive there was some angel peeking over the edge who could see me. I wondered what else they did up there besides look down. When it thundered, my mother used to tell me that the angels were bowling, so obviously they had recreation up there. I wondered if they had to wear those white gowns even when they went bowling. Wouldn't they trip over them or get them dirty? And what about the wings? Wasn't it tough to run with them? And who taught you how to use them? And once you learned, where were you going to go anyway? The thing that bothered me most was that in all the pictures I'd ever seen, angels have blond hair. Did that mean that I couldn't get into heaven, or that I was going to have to spend all of eternity touching up my dark roots? The one basic question was, was heaven going to be the kind of place where I would be comfortable, or the kind of place where nuns would be comfortable?

I could only hope that rock and roll made its way to heaven. I had had enough harp music and Gregorian chant in Catholic school to last me for eternity. If I had to listen to music forever, I hoped it was going to be something I could hum along with. If heaven was the way the nuns described it, it was a pretty dull place. Moreover, the nuns informed us that pets were not allowed in heaven because they have no souls. I was destroyed. I had been planning to spend eternity with my dog at my side. I considered getting the ASPCA after God. But my mother told me that dogs go to "doggie heaven," cats go to "kitty heaven," and so forth. I told her I wanted to go to "doggie heaven." She said that was impossible but that when I got to heaven, I could visit "doggie heaven" whenever I wanted to. That was the best news I'd gotten about heaven. The only thing that makes it worth going there is that the alternatives are even worse. In hell you do nothing but burn. If you are there for lying, your tongue burns. If it's stealing, your hands burn. And if you ate meat on Friday, you probably have eternal heartburn. Purgatory is the same story.

The only place that sounds like any fun at all is limbo. There is no pomp and circumstance about limbo. There are no rules

there because everybody there is pagan and they don't know anything about rules anyway. They just spend all of eternity doing
anything they want to do. They don't have to worry about the
comings and goings of God, or polishing their halos, or taking
harp lessons. There is one drawback, though. No one can figure
out exactly where limbo is. Everybody knows that heaven is "up
there" and hell is "down there" and purgatory is somewhere in
the middle. But where is limbo? Somewhere in the fifth dimension? Wherever it was, Pauli decided that he was going there. He
began his campaign to become a pagan in the summer. While
the rest of us were running through the sprinkler in our bathing
suits, Pauli was running around the block naked. We all stayed
away from him more than usual that summer and kept our pets
clear of him too. We were afraid that at any minute he might
want to offer living sacrifices. The closest he ever came to that
was ripping the lights off lightning bugs and putting them on his
finger like a ring.

   Pauli was determined to convince God that the water they
threw on him when he was a baby was just regular water and not
holy water. I was inclined to believe that. His pagan behavior
was no different than his regular behavior except that he was
making a concerted effort to be irregular. I even put in a word
with God for Pauli's cause. Nobody deserved hell and Pauli's
presence would make some drastic changes in heaven. So it
seemed more merciful to everyone if God would just give Pauli
what he wanted and send him to limbo. Pauli wasn't afraid of
going to the fifth dimension; he spent most of his time there
anyway.

   The nuns did not agree with that. In their eyes, Pauli was not
a pagan. He was a baptized Catholic and therefore ineligible to
go to limbo. Pauli had to shape up fast, but there was no doubt
in their minds that he was incapable of doing it by himself. Nor
did they expect his mother to take responsibility for his behavior.

The nuns always thought that they shouldn't criticize Mrs. Santini because she was a saintly woman. After all, God gave her Pauli and He would only do that to a candidate for sainthood. But Pauli needed help; they got no argument on that point. And they told us that it was up to us to help him.

It was our responsibility as Catholics not only to save our own souls and bear our own guilt, but also that of others. Of course, there was a bonus in it for you. Every soul you saved bought you more points toward heaven. The very first thing you were supposed to do if you saw an accident was baptize any injured person who might die. Baptism is generally something that only a priest should perform; but in extreme circumstances, anybody will do. It was our duty to ensure the baptism of as many people as possible. It seemed to me that the best time to catch them was when they had no choice in the matter; like just before they died or just after they were born. It was better if you spent your whole life Catholic and worrying about your sins; so the nuns impressed upon us the importance of baptizing babies. They were sure that that was what God wanted us to do — make babies and baptize them. And if you were too young to make your own, you had to find one to baptize.

Chapter 8

❦

Pagan Babies

I WAS TOTALLY unprepared for motherhood. I had another brand-new baby sister whose diapers I changed, whom I fed, bathed, and dressed occasionally. But all of this was under my mother's guidance. To have the sole and full-time responsibility for a baby was a terrifying idea. Moreover, I had no means of support and no father for the child. And logic won over the romantic notion of having a baby of my very own to love. I could not do it.

My fears were allayed by the good sisters, who assured me that I didn't have to give the child a father, that financial support wouldn't be a problem. I wouldn't have to care for the baby. And as a matter of fact I wouldn't even have to see the baby. I had serious reservations. But they were older than I, more experienced and certainly conversant with this situation. With no solid reason to do anything else, I decided to defer to their better judgment. And so it was, that at the age of six, I bought my first pagan baby.

By the time I was in fifth grade, I had accumulated eight. For each baby, I had to lay out five bucks. Not all at once, but in ten-cent installments; which may not sound like much. But for a kid, and before inflation, mind you, a dime could go a long way. When penny candy was not a nickel, but two or more pieces for a penny, you could fill a bag with enough root beer barrels licorice, bubble gum, red hot dollars, and BB bats to make it through a matinee. And with fifty dimes, you could ensure hav-ing to buy your clothes in the chubby department. That was quite a sacrifice. And for what?

No one was very clear about exactly what I was getting for those five bucks. I was buying a pagan baby. I really didn't know what "pagan" was or why it made babies marketable. I'd never heard of anybody wanting to buy or sell a regular baby for five dollars. And I didn't get custody, which was a relief. But I'd never get any letters from, or even a picture of this kid. For five dollars, I got no proof that a baby even existed. To me, this was a gyp.

I was certain that I must have been missing something. And yet I was hesitant about raising the question to the nuns. One slip in diplomacy and I would end up sitting on the windowsill with a dunce cap on my head and tape over my mouth, right next to Dianne Luca, who still occupied the spot occasionally. I decided not to risk it. I'd just have to surrender up those dimes and hope that somewhere along the line the reason would become as clear to me as it seemed to be to everyone else.

Pagan babies were the first order of the day—after the pledge of allegiance to the flag and morning prayers, of course. Sister would sit at her desk, front and center, and open the top drawer, where she kept her pagan baby supplies, and tell everyone with pagan baby money to line up in front of the desk. The line had to be straight and silent before she would begin. We all had little booklets. They were seventeen pages long. Each page had three spaces in which we pasted stamps, the size of special edition postage stamps, with pictures of saints on them. Next to the spaces for the stamps was a paragraph about that particular saint. Each stamp cost ten cents. It worked something like green stamps. On those days when I really needed a sugar fix I'd gripe to myself that at least with green stamps you get more for the money and you end up with an appliance or something.

Every morning we lined up to buy our stamps. I'd get one or two and console myself with the thought that my dimes bought me a couple of extra minutes away from schoolwork, a stamp to lick—they tasted pretty good—and a little story to read about some saint while I tried to put the stamp exactly between the lines.

But the ritual ended in the same unpleasant way every day. Sandra Minelli was always the last one in line; partly to show Sister what a good little girl she was to let everyone go ahead of her, and partly to be the grand finale. You see, Sandra brought in at least fifty cents every day and a dollar on Mondays. She got that look of approval from Sister that told the rest of us that some-day our children would be pasting pictures of Sandra Minelli into pagan baby books. And, to make matters worse, when Sister told her that the class would wait while she put her stamps in the book, she magnanimously declined, saying that she would do it during recess—once again a shining example to us all. Given half a chance, the class would have gladly martyred Sandra Minelli and helped her get her picture on that stamp a little sooner.

Sandra became an expert on each and every one of the saints pictured. Those paragraphs whetted her interest enough to make her do extensive research on all their lives. She spent every free moment that did not detract from class time dazzling the nuns with this information. And while the rest of us were working on getting that last stamp into page six, Sandra proudly pasted in her last stamp and coyly asked Sister for another book. Inadvertently, Sandra treated us all to a half hour away from schoolwork. Her accomplishment was the first milestone in the pagan baby drive and therefore reason for ceremony.

Out of the supply drawer came a poster that Sister unrolled and tacked on the bulletin board. It was nearly identical to a picture that hung on the back wall. It was a picture of Jesus Christ sitting on a rock in the middle of a glen, surrounded by playing children, one on His lap, one hanging around His neck; everyone was happy and smiling. Every child in the classroom had fantasies about dissolving into that picture. And every child in that room was chastised at least once that year for turning around in their seats to look at it while we were supposed to be paying attention to Sister. Every time I had to reach under my desk to get a book, I'd turn my head to see Jesus loving children who were neither in a straight line, nor wearing uniforms.

The poster that Sister put in the front of the room was missing a crucial element—the children. It was the very same picture—but, she pointed out the obvious, without the children. We were to supply the children. We were to surround Jesus with our pagan babies lest He be lonely. And which of us could bear the guilt of leaving Jesus alone? Sandra Minelli was the first to offer Him companionship. Her five dollars bought it for Him. For Sandra Minelli's glorification, Sister explained how.

There are millions of babies in this world who are unbaptized and therefore do not know God. That is why there are priests and nuns establishing missions to satiate some of the spiritual starvation that runs rampant. In addition, they work to help these people cope with lives fraught with poverty, pestilence, and disease. Every five dollars that we privileged American

Catholic children send to these missions ensures the baptism of at least one of these pagans. Thus, people who otherwise would end up in limbo get a clear shot at heaven.

I was overwhelmed by the power of those five dollars. I had visions of an infant who, by accident of birth, could expect nothing more than hell on earth, and not even a chance at heaven. It didn't seem fair. And if five dollars from me could change that agony to ecstasy, I was more than happy to give it. I wasn't quite sure how five dollars was going to feed, clothe, and shelter an infant to adulthood, as well as save its immortal soul. Five dollars was a lot of money, but it seemed to me that my parents had already spent more than that on me and I still had a long way to go. Then the thought occurred to me that for the price of one baby, you might be able to save three or four pagan adults. I wondered why nobody else thought of that. Maybe it was because they got done for free. Or maybe it was because they didn't want to be baptized. Maybe they already had their religion. And maybe they only let their babies be baptized because they got clothes and food in the bargain. It seemed entirely possible that they resented someone coming to their country and telling them that their babies were pagan and wanting to change that. Maybe they liked their babies pagan. And maybe that was nobody's business. But maybe they didn't understand about heaven and hell and purgatory and limbo. Neither did I really, but I decided better safe than sorry. And if my five bucks could help some little kid sit on Jesus' lap, I was going to give it.

Despite my good intentions, Sandra Minelli managed to get two pagan babies on the poster before I got my first one. And in the meantime, a few of the other kids had finished their first books as well. So by the time I got to the sheet of pictures, all the good ones had already been cut out, named, and put on the poster. Of course Sandra bought the baby on Jesus' lap. She named it after Sister, wrote Constance Minelli on it, and stuck it on the poster.

By the middle of the year, it was SRO on that poster. Pagan babies begat pagan babies. The guilt inspired by so many Minellis on that poster egged on even the agnostics in the class and absolved the guilt I felt for getting pagan baby money from my father's pocket while he was asleep. If guilt is a cure for apathy, Sandra Minelli is a wonder drug. I got two pagan babies and named one Barbara Ann, for no reason other than I liked the name. The other one I named Roseanne, after my best friend. I would have preferred to let them just keep the names they already had but they couldn't be baptized with pagan names. Somehow I just couldn't name it after myself, as Sandra Minelli did her second one. She did that every year: named the first one after whichever nun was our teacher and the second after herself and subsequent ones after members of her family or friends. I have often been tempted to find out where she is living now and hire a group of people to knock on her door and say, "Hi, we're your pagan babies; Sandra, Sandra, Sandra . . ." I'm sure Sandra is a common name among pagans converted to Catholicism. But even then I didn't believe that they actually changed people's names to suit the whims of children when they baptized them. Especially since there were kids who, even in this, found a way to vent their sadism by naming their babies Ignatious or Aloysius.

Finally the spirit of Christian charity contest was over and Sister tallied the receipts. On Pagan Baby Awards Day I was the proud recipient of two certificates, one for each baby, and a medal of Saint Lucy blessed by our own Father Joseph. Sandra Minelli, far and away the grand prize winner, got herself five certificates, the medal of Saint Lucy, a crucifix, and—the prize we all coveted—a bottle of water from Lourdes. Moreover, thanks to Sandra, our class had two more pagan babies than any other class in the school. And in recognition of this achievement, the nuns bought us the perfect reward for candy-starved children, a class pagan baby.

Chapter 9

∾

Holy Propaganda

THE PAGAN baby drive lasted for three months and during those three months, candy sales at the school store were nil. Nobody dared to buy candy from a nun. They'd been known to confiscate money without even giving as much as a stamp for it. It didn't stop us from eating candy. We brought it from home. After three months of doing it that way, we not only got into the habit but also enjoyed the economical benefits. At Lena's a candy bar cost a nickel. At school it cost a dime. The only difference between the candy bars was age. I knew that aging made a bottle of wine more expensive—but candy bars? I didn't even like my candy bars covered with that white film that aging produces. I'd rather have two shiny, smooth ones than one waxy one. And everybody else felt the same way, except Sandra Minelli, who had given up candy completely.

The nuns had to find a way to move that candy out. Telling us that the profits went to the missions did not boost sales. We'd been supporting the missions without getting candy for three months. Now they wanted us to kick in the price of a second candy bar for every one we bought so they could send money to the missions. And they weren't even offering babies for it this time. Nuns are not real good at salesmanship. They even make heaven look grim; so it is a little unrealistic to expect them to find a way to make moldy candy bars appealing to kids. Besides, it's against their principles to lure people into action. That's the Devil's work. Nonetheless, there were boxes of candy to be sold and they found an honest way to do it—create a demand.

The best way to create an almost insatiable demand for candy is to show a movie. That's exactly what they did. We were so excited when they told us that we were going to spend the afternoon watching a movie, we were willing to buy anything they wanted to sell us. They sat us in the auditorium after lunch and sold us every last piece of candy they had before they turned off the lights. Sister Mary Rose was operating the projector. She was new that year. From the first time we laid eyes on her, we knew she was different. She was younger and prettier than any nun we'd ever seen. But she really won our hearts the day she climbed up and fixed the school bus so we could get home. She was a mechanical whiz. The picture appeared on the screen in perfect focus. It was a picture of the jungle. Great! I loved animal shorts. The camera panned the jungle and came to rest on a piece of barren, parched land. Feet appeared: black, dirt-crusted feet, barely dragging across the ground. The camera moved up and we saw emaciated legs and a crutch. Up further still, and we saw ragged clothes. I began to realize that this short was not going to be a lot of laughs.

The sickly native hobbled up to a ramshackle bamboo hut, struggled to his knees, and laid down his package. Then, with much trouble, he pulled himself to his feet and hobbled off into the jungle. The door to the hut creaked open and a glowing white light appeared. It took a minute to focus my eyes and I saw that the image on the screen was a nun; a nun all dressed in white. She was smiling and she bent down and picked up what the man had left. She uncovered it so that we could see what it was. There, before our eyes, on the silver screen, was a bona fide pagan baby. Not as impressive a sight, perhaps, as the wildlife of the Serengeti Plain; but then we didn't have a vested interest in the Serengeti Plain. Because we sacrificing children sent our five bucks, the nun held the baby close to her spotless white habit and took it inside and closed the door.

The next scene was a little girl, presumably the same pagan baby, receiving her first communion. She was wearing a white dress, just like one I had, and black patent-leather shoes and white anklets, just like mine, courtesy of the missions. She sure had come a long way from being left on the doorstep by a leper. This certainly made it seem well worth the five bucks a shot to buy pagan babies. Some of them even ended up in the movies, which was something I could only dream about.

But as I sat there in the dark, waiting for the feature film to start, and hoping it was a Disney flick, questions started popping into my head. How did those nuns keep their habits bright white? They weren't even dirty around the hem, which trailed along the dusty ground. And what the heck were they always smiling about? Here they were in a place where people were dropping like flies around them from things like malaria, leprosy, and starvation. They lived in bamboo huts, taking care of hundreds of little screaming babies. And heaven only knows what they had to eat. Our nuns lived in a mansion, ate far too much, and took care of healthy, silent children from eight in the morning until three in the afternoon; and they rarely cracked a smile.

The real killer was that our nuns were always touting the missions, always telling us that the greatest vocation anybody could have was to become a missionary. I wished that most of them had become missionaries. I could just imagine them in deepest, darkest Africa with disease and hunger and wild animals and head hunters all around them. If they were grouchy here in the convent with its manicured grounds, and thought that we were little savages, I shuddered to think what their attitude would have been over there. One thing's for sure, the mission compound would have been safer than ever before. Even the most bloodthirsty savage wouldn't tangle with Sister Michael. On the other hand, they wouldn't have gotten many converts, either. Even food, clothes, and shelter wouldn't have been enough to convince anybody to live with Sister Michael. I guess that's why Mother Superior kept her here—to keep things equal. Those kids had to learn to survive their deprivation and we had to learn to survive Sister Michael. Either way, being a Catholic was not much fun.

If you weren't having fun, you were doing it right. You weren't supposed to have fun; you were supposed to sacrifice. That was the point of the mission movie; to show us how much we should be willing to sacrifice and how we should do it happily. I had to admit to myself, though I was ashamed to, that there was no way that I was going to become a missionary. I'd leave the missions to Sandra Minelli. I'd just stay home and pray for the saints; not Sandra Minelli, but the poor pagans who had to put up with her.

The mission movie probably inspired Sandra, but it depressed me. I heaved a sigh of relief when the screen lit up again. Still, after the short—which was not exactly a looney tune—my hopes weren't too high for the feature. But for the sake of Catholic school entertainment and enlightenment, I found that God had gone Hollywood. He brought His *Ten Commandments* down from the Mount to Tinsel Town. Oh, He wasn't in the picture Himself, or even in the credits. He doesn't usually make public appearances. He hires other people to speak on His behalf. They came from all places and all walks of life. So it wasn't surprising that He should find some in Hollywood too. I was sure that Charlton Heston was His modern-day prophet. After all, the Red Sea only parted for one other guy. I thought it was great the way God did that, parted it once so that the Jews could escape from Egypt and once again so that it could be filmed for posterity. Too bad He didn't remember to bring the camera first time around. He could have saved Himself a lot of trouble. But then, I guess Moses was in too big a hurry to take home movies. Besides, Red Sea or not, the whole thing just wouldn't be as impressive a spectacle without the cinemascope and the stereophonic sound.

I was awed. I mean, I always knew it was a great story, but there have been plenty of great stories that have gone nowhere. But consider the writer. Let's face it, His affiliation guarantees success to almost any project. And they did take it on the road first and proved it was a winner. It was an obvious buy for the movies, but whom did they contact? Does God have an agent or did they deal directly with Him? How did they convince Him to do that Red Sea routine again? And what sort of remuneration did He want for His work? We all know that God is not into money. He does, however, have several charities under His name. Maybe He deferred His payment to them. Or maybe they sent the checks directly to Rome, where His overhead is quite high. Whatever the cost was, the movie was well worth it.

I learned a lot from that movie that the nuns would never have told us. All we ever heard about from them was the suffering that God demanded—and granted there was plenty of that too. But there are other things in life. They just don't understand how difficult it is to get most people involved in a story about a six-hundred-year-old man who spends his life wandering around the desert and never gets where he's going anyway. But take the same man, make him good-looking, let him fall in love a couple of times, make his nemesis good-looking, and you've got a story that people will remember. The hero is a sympathetic character, someone with whom everyone can identify. He has feelings and weaknesses and strengths just like the rest of us. That burning bush is a shocker to him in the beginning too. It took Hollywood to bring the story down to earth for me and make it believable.

The movie was so good that we forgot how rotten the candy was. We even forgot how depressing the mission short was. We were totally engrossed in what was happening on the screen. When the Red Sea parted, we all cheered and somebody yelled, "Go Moses!" Sister Michael stood up and insisted that the projector be stopped so that she could impress upon us that this was not a sports event but a learning experience. She threatened us to behave accordingly. The movie continued playing to a silent audience. Though the picture didn't quite jibe with the nuns' rendition of the story, they were nonetheless happy about the fact that it did stimulate our interest in the Bible. Because of that, they kept those Bible pictures coming. We saw them all: *The Ten Commandments, The Bible, The Story of Ruth, The Song of Bernadette, The Shoes of the Fisherman,* all preceded by the mission shorts. Not exactly what one might call lighthearted entertainment, especially not to the under-ten-year-old crowd; but it was as lighthearted as we got and it was entertainment. I'd take an afternoon with Charlton Heston over one with Sister Michael any day!

≈

Chapter 10

Martyrmania

A S I got older, I began to realize that those movies we were seeing were meant to be Catholic training films. That realization turned me off to my favorite movie, *Quo Vadis*. That's the one where Deborah Kerr falls in love with Robert Taylor. After a really steamy romance, their love conquers the Roman Empire and they ride off into the sunset together. But according to the nuns, I missed the main thrust—the persecution of the Christians. They were crucified, burned, eaten by lions, and thereby transformed into martyrs. I suppose the reason that didn't impress me as the central theme was because I had my eyes closed during most of those parts. I'm funny that way; I'm not crazy about watching people get mutilated. That wasn't the point that the nuns were trying to make either. But you did have to watch the people being martyred in order to see that they were doing it with smiles on their faces. While I thought that was nuts, Sister thought it was not only noble but required.

I hadn't even begun to live when they hit us with the news that we were supposed to be willing to die for our religion. And the way they told the story, they made it sound as though it were a definite possibility for each and every one of us. Another reason for me to feel guilty. Nonetheless, I determined early on that if someone decided to start rounding up Catholics with the intention of doing away with them, they weren't going to get me. I knew exactly how I would play it.

"Are you a Catholic?"

"No. I'm a kid."

"A Catholic kid?"

"No. An American kid."

"A Catholic American kid?"

"No. A cute American kid."

If they pushed it any further, or if they managed to get a copy of my baptism certificate before I had a chance to get out of the country, they were going to have to take me kicking and screaming. Dignity was out and so were smiling and singing. If I was going to be an hors d'oeuvre for a lion just because somebody threw water on me without my consent, I wasn't going to pretend to be happy about it.

What really had me worried was that the nuns seemed to be expecting or at least hoping that the persecution would start any day. They grilled us, trying to impress upon us that we should go happily because by the time the lion burped, we'd be in heaven. The only thing they impressed upon me was an acute fear of lions. I refused to go to the circus. The Ringling Brothers were promising the time of your life, but I'll bet that's how Circus

Maximus started too. I became leery of the zoo as well. Maybe the nuns were right; the conspiracy was beginning. It looked innocent enough on the surface, simple entertainment. But behind it all I knew there was some pagan who was working to accumulate lions and then, before you know it, it's *Quo Vadis* all over again.

Staying away from lions wasn't enough to guarantee safety, though. Certainly Circus Maximus and the lions were all the rage for a while there. But there were audiences who preferred the more subdued show, or who could not afford to import lions. In which case, there were crucifixions; also burning at the stake, beheading, disembowelment, dismemberment, and a multitude of other imaginative means to the same end. We heard about each and every one in explicit detail. I couldn't even smile through the explanation of these things and that proved to me beyond a shadow of a doubt that I wouldn't be smiling if it really happened.

While I was busy trying to keep my lunch down through these rather grim fairy tales, Sandra Minelli egged Sister on. That girl was determined to be a card-carrying saint by hook or by crook and martyrdom looked like the quickest way for her to get there. She wanted to learn everything she could about it. There is only one catch: if you let that smile fade for even one minute, you might have to do time in purgatory for a show of weakness in faith. As if that weren't tough enough, in order to go straight to heaven, you also had to sing, preferably some snappy Gregorian chant tune. I was sure that, given the chance, Sandra could pull it off. She was the only person I have ever known who could sing Gregorian chant at age eleven. I was equally sure that while Sandra was singing her swan song, I would be playing jump rope under an assumed name in some South American country, a fugitive from martyrdom.

Despite the fact that I spent a great deal of time plotting my escape from the lions, I did wonder how many graces toward heaven I was accumulating by being forced to listen to the horrors. There were even those days when I would have thrown myself to a lion just so I wouldn't have to hear about even worse tortures. The worst of all was the saint whose intestines were attached to a pole and he was forced to walk around it until he disemboweled himself and died. I couldn't understand that. Why didn't he just sit down and say forget it? What could they have done—killed him? I guess the reason he kept walking was to get into heaven, smiling and singing all the way.

As if listening to these stories didn't have enough impact on kids, there were pictures on the walls to illustrate the stories. While kids in public school were looking at Picasso prints, we had pictures of Jesus with his heart in his hand, or being cruci-fied, Joan of Arc smiling through the flames, and others meeting similar ends. This did give us an edge in one area, though. On Saturday afternoons while Pauli was hiding under the theater seat, making foul noises and spitting jujubees, I was enjoying the picture. Frankenstein, Dracula, the Wolfman, and their peers were rather docile and likeable fellows compared to the perse-cuting pagans we'd been hearing about. Horror movies scared the life out of Pauli, but for me they were happy-go-lucky enter tainment. Let's face it, what's so frightening about being bitten on the neck by a vampire compared with being disemboweled?

The nuns never ran out of grisly stories. If they weren't telling us about someone dying a gruesome death, they were telling us about someone with stigmata. It's not a disease, but it is as bad as it sounds. Stigmata are the wounds of Christ; the holes in the hands, feet, and side that bleed. People who get stigmata are practically canonized while still alive. The Church takes it as a sign from God that the person is blessed. I was amazed by how excited the nuns got about bleeding. It was a terrible disappoint-ment to me when I got a bloody nose one day and all I got for it was an ice pack. As I was laying there on the couch in the nurse's office I wondered how I could get stigmata. If my hand bled instead of my nose, the nuns would not only stay off my back but they would go out of their way to be nice to me. It never hurts to make friends with people destined for greatness.

The only way I was going to get stigmata was to give them to myself. I wasn't sure I had the courage, but that seemed to be the price of glory. Of course, self-inflicted stigmata might not get me into heaven but it would keep me out of hell on earth. I wasn't nearly as worried about dealing with God as I was about dealing with the nuns. Stigmata would give me real leverage with them. Still, I wasn't as crazy about pain as they were. The answer was makeup. My mother had plenty of it. I got her tube of bright red lipstick and drew a circle on the palm of each of my hands. I stared at them for a long while and even I wasn't convinced. Besides, they had to be open sores that bled from time to time. They also had to go straight through the hands.

Even fear of the nuns couldn't convince me that it was worth driving a nail through my hands. But what stopped me, more than the pain, was what I knew would be my mother's reaction.

"Mom, look, stigmata!"

She'd crack up and shake her head and say, "You are a weird kid."

Even if it was real, my mother's reaction would be, "Cute joke, but if you don't stop it now, you're going to go live at the convent with the nuns."

The nuns may have been happy about stigmata, but my mother would not allow them in her house. She disapproved of putting holes in the human body. I wasn't even allowed to have pierced ears. On that point, the sisters agreed with my mother. The day Dianne appeared at school with freshly pierced ear-lobes, Sister stood her up in front of the class and lectured on the sinfulness of desecrating the body. She ended in usual fash-

ion with, "Now, young lady, what have you got to say for yourself?"

Any one of the rest of us would have burst into tears. Not
Dianne. She answered, almost innocently, "I only did it to make
sure I could handle stigmata."

The class broke out in laughter, and Dianne was marched off
to the principal's office. Dianne would never be a martyred
Catholic; but she lived in constant threat of being martyred *by*
the Catholics.

~

Chapter 11

How Do You Know You've Been Blessed with a Baby and Other Religious Questions the Nuns Wouldn't Answer

BECAUSE I tried my best not to think about martyrdom, the nuns escaped my usual barrage of questions on that subject. But without even trying, I did come up with one. Why did the lions eat the Christians? In the Abraham and Isaac story, God was content to find that Abraham was willing to sacrifice his son at His command, and He didn't let him actually go through with it. It would seem that once God saw the Christians go willingly into the arena and keep singing even when the lions were released, He wouldn't actually make them go through with it, either. Besides, wouldn't it have been more just and also a better show of His power if the lions spared the Christians and ate the Romans instead? That way, the faithful survive to spread His word and the wicked are punished.

Sister's answer was, "That is not the way the Lord works. And it is not for us to question His actions. Faith in Him is the only way we will get to heaven."

Okay, so she didn't know the answer to that one. But there were times I asked questions for which they did have the answer and wouldn't give it. In first grade when we were discussing "Go forth, be fruitful and multiply," Sister told us that God made men and women so they would get married and be together and when God saw that they were deserving, He would bless them with a baby.

I raised my hand and asked what I thought was the obvious question. "How do you know when you've been blessed?" I was hoping that the answer would be that God sent an angel to tell you just like He did with Mary. But I didn't think that that was the case because I remember when my mother told my father that my first sister was coming she didn't mention any angels. Moreover, my father didn't seem surprised. Maybe the angel told him. But he didn't mention any angels either. And if you want my opinion, the angel would have been the high point of that story. It was something else that told them that they'd been blessed.

Sister's answer was, "When the time comes, you just know."

Terrific—being blessed with a baby was just as mysterious as getting "the calling." The nuns wouldn't tell how they got the calling, but my mother couldn't keep a secret. She'd been blessed with babies so I was sure she could tell me how it happened. I asked her. And she told me. It didn't sound like any blessing to me. It sounded to me as though they did it themselves. The next day I told Sister my conclusions. She still insisted that they couldn't have gotten a baby without God. But my mother didn't mention anything about His being there and that's not the kind of thing that she would leave out of the story. He must have done it long distance. And there was something else too: if they couldn't get a baby without God, God couldn't get one without them either. I told Sister how I felt about that too. She called it "carrying out God's will."

If being fruitful and multiplying is God's will, why is there so much talk about its being sinful? And since God was the one who designed the whole baby-making system in the first place, why didn't He make it less controversial? And if it is God's will for us to be fruitful and multiply, why are the nuns defying that will by taking a vow of celibacy? The answer I got was that I was too young to understand. Apparently God's will is quite complex. I wondered how even He could keep track of what He wanted. He's worse than a kid writing a Christmas list. One minute He wants you not to eat meat on Fridays and the next thing you know, He decides that it's okay. I wondered how many sins I'd committed without even knowing it. If there are rules to govern your eating habits then there must be rules that pertained to other daily functions as well, like going to the bathroom. There had to be rules about that because we had to raise our hands to be able to go at all. The nuns usually let us go alone but they made it clear that God was watching. So embarrassing! Doesn't He have better things to do with His time?

God spends His time watching everything. He knows all. What a mind! Nothing escapes Him. I had trouble jumping rope double dutch because I had to think about two things going at once. God can focus on an infinite number of things. Not only can He pick any person on Earth at random and tell you off the top of His head when that person was born, when he will die, and all the sins he's committed during his lifetime, but also something as trivial as how many hairs there are on his head. He's better than Kreskin. Of course He could be faking the number of hairs just for the dramatic effect. I really didn't care how many hairs were on my head as long as there were a lot. What happens when a hair falls out? If it is really important to Him to keep a tally of how many hairs are on all the heads of all the people in the world, He must get really tense in the morning when everybody is brushing their hair. All the numbers change. If I were God, I'd appreciate bald people.

As I got older, my questions got a little more sophisticated. I knew where babies came from, but I started to worry about where we, collectively, came from. I'd heard the story of the creation of the world thousands of times, but something wasn't clicking. You've got Adam and Eve. And they have Cain and Abel. Cain kills Abel. And here we all are. Evolution? Absolutely not. Then how did Adam, Eve, and Cain populate the world? They couldn't have done it alone without committing a sin. For Adam and Eve's children to multiply, they had to marry out of their immediate family.

This led me to assume that God had actually created two or three pairs of Adams and Eves and scattered them around the Earth strategically so that their offspring could procreate. That made sense to me. Sister said that I was wrong. There was only one Adam and Eve. And their offspring alone populated the entire world. Dianne Luca asked the question that I thought but didn't dare verbalize, "Who'd sleep with Cain?"

Coming from anyone else, that question would have flipped Sister out. But she was glad to see that Dianne knew the difference between good and bad and answered that Cain reformed and went on to become a good husband and father.

But he still had to be married to a sibling and I asked if that wasn't committing a sin. Sister's explanation was that that was before it was a sin. Again God changed the rules. How are we supposed to keep up with Him? Does He send out a newsletter or what?

Nuns and priests are there to keep us up to date with what

God wants from us. Nearly every line of questioning I took with the nuns ended with their saying, "Because God wants it that way." Who told them that?! Not a burning bush. That only happened once and it was so spectacular, they still talk about it. And as I recall, the burning bush had only ten requests. But the nuns had an answer to everything and their conclusions were always backed up by, "God wants it that way." Now as far as I know, God hasn't directly spoken to anybody in years. So how does anybody know that God wants girls in Catholic school to wear their skirts below the knee? Moreover, if someone was fortunate enough to have the opportunity to have a conversation with God, wouldn't they find more profound issues to discuss with Him than fashion?

During religion class, I tried to stay away from questions about God's will. Church history seemed to be a safer subject and certainly one the nuns enjoyed discussing. They loved to tell us about the popes. The popes were a pretty boring lot except that they lived in a huge palace, wore better jewelry than Elizabeth Taylor, and were always dressed in fancy clothes and great hats, and had names like Leo and Linus. Popes spend most of their time thinking about God and if they do it real well, they go into ecstasy. Ecstasy is one of the few holy things that is not bloody and it's probably a lot of fun for the guy who does it. But it seemed gross to have to watch it. One pope used to do it at the dinner table. While everyone else was eating, he used to think about God and he got so carried away that he used to rise up right off his chair. My parents would kill me if I did something weird like that at the dinner table. And I could see why. How can anybody eat with someone floating around the table?

I'd had enough of the supernatural stuff. I was more interested in the human aspects of the history of the Church. I wanted to know exactly why Martin Luther got kicked out.

"He was critical of the Holy Father."

"What did he say?"

"Among other things, he accused the Holy Father of selling blessings."

"Why did he do that?"

"Because the Church was in desperate need of money and the Holy Father was blessing those who contributed to the Church."

"Oh." Now, we'd been told that a papal blessing was a ticket to heaven. I could understand why the pope would be grateful to anyone who gave money to the Church, particularly in times of greater need. However, it seemed to me that there were plenty of poor people who would have contributed gladly if they'd had the money, yet they were not getting his blessing. You only got the blessing if you had money and gave that money to the Church. It seemed understandable to me that Martin Luther might construe the pope's blessing people who gave money as selling the blessings. I think the whole thing could have been avoided if, in order to raise the money for the Church, the pope gave some of his jewelry to the rich people for the money they gave him. Martin Luther certainly couldn't have criticized him for selling jewelry.

It really is too bad that the Church could never close the rift between itself and Martin Luther. He was only trying to be fair. And in the end, the Church did consider his point of view. Now when the Church needs money, they don't give blessings for it; they pass the collection plate, raffle Cadillacs, sell pagan babies, and have bingo games. If the Church and Martin Luther had worked together on it, they could have invented bingo a lot sooner. My only complaint with bingo is that kids aren't allowed to play. You have to spend a lifetime proving you are a good Catholic before you are granted the privilege of sitting in on the bingo games. It must be worth it, though, because every Wednesday night, everybody's grandmother gets dressed up for a hot night of bingo. Bingo games are never scheduled during "Lawrence Welk." The Church knows how to hold on to its audience.

They really learned from the Martin Luther incident. That blunder cost them thousands of followers. I know it bothered them because they still hate to talk about it. Still, they insisted that ours was the one true faith and anybody who wasn't smart enough to see that was going to have a tougher time getting into heaven. And so was anyone who ever tried to defy the pope again. We were not to question the pope. He was infallible.

Dianne Luca asked the obvious question. "But what if he makes a mistake?"

"He doesn't," Sister said emphatically, "he's infallible. That means he's incapable of making a mistake."

The popes may be infallible, but they change their minds as often as God does. For instance, it was a pope's idea that priests take a vow of celibacy. It wasn't always that way. Popes used to be married and even have children. As a matter of fact, Lucrezia Borgia was the daughter of the pope who started celibacy vows. Now if that wasn't a mistake, I don't know what is. I'd heard rumors about Lucrezia and her marital problems, specifically that she had a talent for losing husbands. Rumor had it that while Columbus was busy discovering America, Lucrezia was busy discovering the uses of poison. That was another subject that the nuns wouldn't talk about. Their silence on the subject led me to believe that Lucrezia must have been even worse than I suspected. I surmised that the pope decided to become celibate in order not to have children, particularly bad children like Lucrezia Borgia.

No matter how the nuns tried to squelch it, the subject of violence in the Church kept surfacing. One day I asked what the Inquisition was and was told that that would be explained to me later—much later. Sister said that I was far too young to be expected to understand a subject as complex as the Inquisition.

If Sister thought that we were too young to hear about it, it must have been unspeakable. I couldn't handle the things that they thought we *should* understand, like martyrdom and stigmata. I was still trying to figure out how that white wafer became the body of Christ or why holy water was holy. Heaven, hell, purgatory, and limbo confused me endlessly. It got to the point that I was grateful to the nuns for what they didn't tell me.

I didn't even have to voice my lack of understanding—the nuns could read it on my face. The nuns spent their entire day looking over a sea of glazed faces. Our class pictures looked like a wax museum scene with Sandra Minelli smiling in the middle to show how lifelike we all were compared to real kids. It was obvious how confused we were. Sister assured us that our lack of understanding was perfectly normal. Only saints can fully comprehend the dogma of the Church; the best the rest of us could do was pray for knowledge to come to us. I prayed like crazy for knowledge—especially during tests. I never solved one mathematical equation with prayers nor did I develop an understanding of either Lucrezia Borgia or celibacy. Prayer did not make me any more willing to be a martyr. It simply wasn't working for me. But there was an answer for that too. Sometimes prayers take a long time to be answered. Saint Helena prayed for forty years until her son reformed. Unfortunately they didn't give us forty years to take a math test. And my attention span was too short to wait forty years or longer for the answer to any question. Nonetheless, the nuns kept us praying.

Chapter 12

❧

The Rosary in under Fifteen Minutes

THE FIRST and worst subject of the afternoon was the rosary. It took anywhere from twenty minutes to half an hour, depending on who was leading the prayers. When it was Sandra Minelli's turn, you could bank on a half hour of piety. Sandra loved center stage, particularly when playing to an impressive audience like God and Sister. She performed each prayer with the same dramatic flair that she brought to her poetry recitations. It was only her reverence for the rosary that kept Sister from applauding, as it was our fear of Sister that kept us from throwing rotten fruit, or just throwing up.

Everyone else did their best to get through it as quickly as possible, though some weren't too successful. The same kids that couldn't say things like, "big black bugs bleed black blood," three times fast, were also incapable of saying the Hail Mary ten times fast. It takes a while to get the cadence, and to make sure that every syllable is spoken clearly. But we did get plenty of practice. In no time at all, I could say, "HailMaryfullofgrace-theLordiswiththeeblessedartthouamongwomenandblessedisthe-fruitofthywombJesus," as easily as I could say, "supercalifragilis-ticexpialidocious," even though I didn't understand it as well. "Fruit of thy womb Jesus?" Fruit! How did fruit get into this? Fruit, daily bread, Last Supper, fasting, children starving in China. It seemed to me that we were awfully preoccupied with food. It took about ten million Hail Marys before I realized that the fruit was only figurative. I also understood the facts of life for years before I knew what "thy womb Jesus" was. It sounds pretty blood and guts to a little kid. I just took it for granted that it was some sort of reference to what happened to Jesus and I didn't want the nuns to regale me with the specifics.

It was during a Christmas pageant, when the nuns decided to include not only the wise men, the shepherds, and the nativity, but also a reenactment of the events leading up to it, that I finally understood the Hail Mary. The first part of the prayer was the message that the angel Gabriel brought from God to Mary to tell her that she had been blessed with a baby and to name him Jesus. Why did we keep repeating God's message back to Him? Was it to remind Him that Mary was a virgin, the same way the nuns were adamant about making that point to us? Didn't God get a little bored listening to the same words over and over? Wouldn't He have appreciated hearing some new material? Ours may not have been the most refined prayers in the world, but I think God would have been overjoyed with the effort. I couldn't understand how the nuns, who were so firm about not repeating themselves, did nothing but repeat things to God. If I were He, my intelligence would be insulted. Hearing the same routine over and over has to have about the same effect on the sensibilities as watching reruns of "The Beverly Hillbillies."

I figured that saying the rosary was more for Sister's benefit than for God's. Everybody has their own way of killing half an hour. Some people needlepoint, some do crossword puzzles, some take a walk: nuns do the rosary. From what we saw, they didn't have much fun. So if they enjoyed a good rosary recitation, the least we could do was humor them. Besides, we had no choice. But there was a limit to my benevolence. If I was going to do it, I was going to try my damnedest to get it over as quickly as possible. It's not that difficult to speed up prayers. You just recite a half beat faster than everyone else. It doesn't take long for the rest of them to get up the courage to join the cause. You must, however, accelerate gently or Sister will put the brakes on the whole project and see to it that the rosary takes forty-five minutes. Nuns never stop prayers, even to reprimand. What they do is pray more loudly and slowly; and it takes even less effort for a nun to squelch a revolution than for a kid to incite one.

I set a goal for myself. I was going to break the fifteen-minute rosary. It wasn't easy, since the only way you can really make time is when you're leading. My turn only came around once a month. That gave me nine rosaries a year to work out the pacing and go for it. There were also several variables to be considered. First and foremost was how pious Sister decided to be on that given day. Piety proportionately decreases speed. The second was the general disposition of the class. The more antsy they were, the easier it was to speed them up. Then there was the pacing. I said the first half of the prayer, then everyone, including me, responded. If I started too fast, Sister would slow it up immediately. But if I started too slowly, I would never be able to make up the time. I'll never forget my best day. It was practically

handed to me. Everything was perfect. Sister had the flu, Sandra
Minelli was absent, it was a rainy day and we had to stay inside
for recess, so everyone was restless. I started a little more quickly
than usual, counting on the flu to control Sister. The rest of the
class moved along without prompting. I got through the first
decade in three minutes ten seconds. Unbelievable time. Four
more to go. I kept the pace steady through the second and third,
then stepped it up a little in the fourth. I clocked in after the
fourth at ten minutes forty-five seconds. One to go. I kept fighting the urge to be greedy and tried to stay consistent. I was too
close to risk pushing it. Amen. Thirteen minutes thirty-seven
seconds. Record time. My finest hour. It compensated for the
many disappointments. Out of nine rosaries a year for nine
years—eighty-one rosaries—I may have broken fifteen minutes
half a dozen times. And if you consider that we said the rosary
every single day, say twenty a month, nine months a year for nine
years—1,620 rosaries—bringing in six in under fifteen minutes
is a depressing proportion. If we say the average rosary took
twenty minutes, we spent 32,400 minutes or 540 hours saying
the rosary. Did you ever stop to think what twenty-five people
could accomplish in 540 hours? That's over thirteen work weeks.

That time was not wasted, we were assured. According to the
nuns, we were not just sitting there, repeating words we didn't
understand—we were praying for causes. If someone had a special cause, like a sick relative, we would devote the rosary to
that. Nuns are always on the lookout for unfortunate situations
so we were never at a loss for things to which we could devote a
rosary. We said rosaries for everything from peace on earth to
Sister's, cousin's, wife's, brother's hangnail. Once a week, we
were all supposed to pick someone in purgatory to pray for.
Great! I didn't know if anyone I knew was in purgatory. They
don't publish lists. It was Sister's contention that it was a fairly
safe bet that anyone we knew who had died without their scapu-

lar—hardly the first thing you check—was doing time in purgatory. And if by chance they'd been sprung, God would deflect your prayers to someone else's case. Every prayer said for a soul in purgatory helped shorten his term of confinement. When we prayed for souls in purgatory, I always asked God to put my good intentions toward the release of the one with the longest sentence and the fewest people pleading his case. When we were allowed to pray for our own intentions, I was far less altruistic. One of my favorite requests was, "Dear Lord, please make Sister disappear." I used to goad Him: "Come on, you can do it, a guy who parted the Red Sea. She's just a small nun. I'll tell you what, you don't even have to keep her for good; just till we're on the bus. It would be the biggest thrill she's had in years; being part of a miracle. They'd probably even make her a saint for it." She never disappeared. I think I blew my chances by bringing up the saint business. I had a pretty solid case until then. But God's not into those flashy miracles anymore. I didn't honestly expect He would do it anyway. The fantasy gave me something more to do than just play with my rosaries.

The nuns do not approve of playing with rosary beads. At least that's what they told us. But next to candy, rosary beads were the hottest item at the school concession store. Their marketing strategy of this item was brilliant. It was mandatory that all students have rosary beads. Rosary beads were, along with holy medals, deregulated. The tenure of rosary beads and medals was the only evidence that we were not a socialist society. We capitalistic children became obsessed with the acquisition of rosary beads. There were tiny beads or extra large ones; round beads or oval; pink, blue, black, rhinestones, even crystal. By the middle of the year, we had accumulated every make and model of rosary beads on the market and our parents were getting tired of investing. Except Sandra Minelli's parents, who would gladly have mortgaged their house to help Sandra corner the rosary bead market. The school store could not, however, survive on Sandra's patronage alone. Sales had leveled off and began slipping. The 10-percent-off sale caused no more than a ripple. They needed something big. And they found it—glow-in-the-dark rosaries to facilitate prayer in dark places.

They had to reorder the first week. We spent our entire recess period standing in line to get the new, improved rosary beads. The nuns put a two per customer limit on them, because there were kids buying four or five pairs and selling them at a profit to other kids in their neighborhood whose Catholic schools hadn't introduced them yet, or to Catholic kids who went to public schools. They were even selling to Protestant kids, some of whom wanted to convert after seeing the trappings of Catholicism. There was a near riot at Saint Lucy's store when the last pair of fluorescent rosaries was sold. The girl who bought them barely escaped with her life, much less the beads. It would be at least a month before the next shipment would arrive.

During that time, my one and only pair—my parents refused to spring for more—broke. I was ashamed to admit it, even to myself, but I was glad they had broken. It wasn't my fault. I didn't do it on purpose. So there was nothing to feel guilty about. And now I could take the beads off and string them up and make a glow-in-the-dark necklace and matching bracelet. If only they hadn't broken in school, on the playground, with Sister standing right there! I had fallen down and the beads came out of my pocket and had somehow gotten mangled as badly as I had. Sister came over to offer aid and comfort. She took the broken beads out of my hands and assured me that they would have a proper burial. Then she sent me to the school nurse to have her tend to my bloodied knee and elbow. To this day, I'm sure that nun is wearing a glow-in-the-dark necklace under her habit.

The burial ground for religious articles is not a hoax. There really is, at every convent, at least a small piece of hallowed ground where the nuns bury things. Like children? Roseanne was convinced of it. When the boarders decided that they were going to go out and investigate the piece of ground that was off limits to everyone, Roseanne was a reluctant accomplice. She went with the understanding that all she would have to do was hold the flashlight. She watched as the other girls dug up a broken statue; obviously the murder weapon. Then some shreds of cloth; the victim's clothes. She dropped her flashlight and ran; she'd seen enough. No amount of reasoning with her would dissuade her of her macabre conclusions. When Sister brought a skeleton into science class one day, Roseanne was sure she knew where Sister had gotten it. That day when we said the rosary, Roseanne devoted two decades to the skeleton, and three that she not meet the same end. I doubt that the skeleton ever got to heaven; Catholic school was as close as he could get. But, to the best of my knowledge, Roseanne is not buried in a shallow grave behind the convent. No matter how slowly you say it, the rosary will almost always work when you pray for the probable.

Chapter 13

The Dashboard
Navigator

ALL OF our praying was done in front of statues. We didn't have to go out of our way to find a statue—you couldn't spit in Catholic school without hitting one. The nuns told us that the purpose of all the statues was so that the saints could look over us and protect us. For people who seemed intent on having us die for our faith, it seemed odd that they should invest in so much protection. It wasn't inconsistent, though. If somebody wanted to round up Catholics in order to martyr them, all those statues would tell them where to find us; martyred thus, we'd go straight to heaven. And in the meantime, they would protect us from accidents. They did a good job. Nobody ever had an accident on school grounds. I wondered how much credit should go to the saints and how much should go to the fact that you can't have many accidents sitting with your hands folded on the desk.

Statues must have had some protective powers, because people put them in their cars and felt more secure. My grandmother did. And I loved going places with her; not only because she was an expert on candy stores and ice cream parlors, but also because I felt safe in her car. We traveled in the company of Jesus, Mary, and Christopher. Jesus and Mary stood in two circular dents in the dashboard. All the cars I'd seen had these two indentations—minimum safety standards, two saints. Among the many options in my grandmother's car was the added safety feature of the extra saint. Christopher stood between Mary and Jesus, a quarter of an inch taller. He never fell off the dashboard, despite the fact that he was not as securely anchored as the others, and my grandmother never had an accident. It might have had something to do with the fact that my grandmother usually drove at a rip-roaring speed of thirty-five miles an hour. My father's car had the indentations, but no saints. I always wondered if he drove the way he did because there were no saints, or if the saints had jumped out when they saw the way he drove.

When I was young, almost all the cars in my neighborhood had saints. Different cars had different saints. Naturally I assumed that the status of the saint had to be equal to the status of the car he protected. Cadillacs got Jesus; Oldsmobiles got Mary; Chevys, Joseph; and Volkswagens needed Christopher. Of course you could buy the saints separately as well. But if your saint was occupied elsewhere and you happened to get into an accident, did you send the car to the shop to repair the fender and the Jesus? Rolls-Royces are obviously pagan cars; not only because they are the epitome of decadence, but because their protectors, who are outside and not looking over the well-being of the driver, are most certainly not saints. They are winged pagan idols. No doubt they protect the physical well-being of the car's occupants, but at the expense of their souls. We had no Rolls-Royces in our neighborhood. We were all good Catholics.

If you must venerate a statue, it has got to bear the papal seal of approval. Golden calves are out. But then, so is Christopher. So before you go melting down your gold jewelry to make statues, you'd better check through the current catalog of saints to find out who's in. Statues of beings with a fire burning in their bellies are heretical. However, a patron saint with a votive candle is not only in good taste but also an irrefutable display of holiness. And of course the next best thing to being in heaven is living in a house that is decorated with medieval piety. They are easy to recognize; they are the ones with the Saint Francis of Assisi birdbath on the front lawn and the Blessed Mother next to the steps. Inside, it's the economy version of the Vatican, miniature *Pietà* and all.

The nuns used to feel right at home in Sandra Minelli's house. The Minellis had almost as many statues as the convent and plenty of holy pictures too. Mrs. Minelli used to invite nuns over for dinner all the time. She was comfortable with them because her sister was a nun. I think her sister was also her interior decorator. Not only was the place loaded with religious paraphernalia, but the furniture was designed to discourage people from overexposing their bodies, particularly on hot days when there was an increased temptation to do so. The couch and chairs were covered with plastic. If you sat on the Minellis' couch with too much skin showing, chances were that you would lose that skin. Not only did you have to peel yourself off the furniture, but everyone in the room could hear you doing it.

We never played at Sandra Minelli's house, since you never knew when you might run into a nun and we got enough of them at school. Besides, Sandra didn't play much. She spent most of her time doing reports on the missions, or building shrines for her mother's statues. Once, Pauli went over to her house and told her he would help her build a shrine. They got all their art supplies together and sat on the couch to work on the coffee table. When Sandra left the room for a minute, Pauli smeared some airplane glue on the plastic where she was sitting. Sandra came back and sat down long enough to glue herself to the couch. Not only did Sandra fail to reform Pauli, she also blew her saintly image by smacking him on the head. Because of the threat he posed to Sandra's sainthood, and also because he drew a mustache on the statue of the Blessed Mother, Pauli was not allowed to play at the Minelli house anymore.

I was no more interested in building shrines than Pauli was. We did have some statues in our house, but most of them were of animals. The only one that looked as though it had something to do with biblical times was on my father's desk. It wasn't The Sacred Heart, or The Child of Prague, or Our Lady of Fatima. It was called *The Rape of the Sabines.* And not only were the people missing halos, they were missing their clothes as well. It was obviously a statue to which only a pagan would kneel. But even Sister said that it was all right to have it around the house. It was art. As long as nobody built a shrine for it or prayed to it, there was no problem. Even God appreciated art.

At school, however, both art and history took a back seat to holy statues. On our eighth grade class trip, we went to Washington, D.C. After we did the Capitol and the White House and drove past the Washington Monument and the Lincoln Memorial, we took a vote on what to do next—the Smithsonian or the religious wax museum. The vote came out eighteen for the Smithsonian, four for the religious wax museum. A landslide; we went to the wax museum. The four votes for the wax museum were the heavies: the three nuns who were chaperoning and Sandra Minelli.

We drove down a back street to a modest white building. The

place was crawling with nuns. All those black habits swarming around the place accentuated the white stucco walls of the building. It was unnerving. They didn't pay any attention to us. For a change, even our own sisters weren't hovering around us. They reminded us—threatened actually—to be quiet and respect-ful, and off they went.

Roseanne and I were the last ones in. It was dark and dank; the perfect place for the creature from the black lagoon to live. The first scene was, appropriately enough, Adam and Eve hang-ing onto their fig leaves while they hightailed it out of the Garden. We gave it a glance as we sauntered by. It wasn't until we got to Moses that we realized that we had been missing part of the novelty of the scenes. They had little talk boxes just like at the zoo. Only you didn't need a little elephant key to work them. All you had to do was press a button. Roseanne pushed it and we listened to the voice of God recite the ten commandments to Moses, who was kneeling in front of the burning bush that flick-ered just like my grandmother's artificial fireplace.

The Joan of Arc scene flickered the same way. She was smil-ing and her voice praised God until death when we pressed the button on the box. It would have been really sickening if those statues had been even the least bit lifelike. God, in wax, is par-ticularly unimpressive. He really lacked charisma, not to men-tion credibility. The statue would have made a great novelty item, if it only had a wick. It would have been the perfect sou-venir for my mother, who had a thing for candles. Of course I'd feel hesitant about burning God, even a bad likeness. But a Joan of Arc candle would be all right. Everybody's burned her.

While I was busy coming up with a new concept in votive candles, the nuns were flitting around the wax museum like they'd died and gone to heaven. They had a great time with the voice boxes too. I even saw some of them push the same one twice. The last exhibit was the Last Supper. That one practically made them swoon; twelve holy men in one place. They overlooked the presence of Judas. It was time to start home, but they could barely pry themselves away. This was the closest they were going to get to saints for a while. They wanted the moment to linger a little longer.

There was a gift shop in the museum and we all stopped in to pick up memorabilia. The nuns bought postcards to bring back to the convent to impress their fellow nuns with the celebrities they'd seen. Sandra Minelli bought another statue for her mother's collection. I bought a couple of postcards, partly because Sister Michael was taking note of who was interested, and partly to prove to my mother that I was telling the truth when I told her why we missed the Smithsonian. She thought that I made up these stories. I was flattered that she gave me credit for such a vivid imagination. I was more than a little disappointed that I'd gone all the way to Washington and didn't get to the Smithsonian, but I tried to comfort myself with the thought that I'd done something original. Not many people go to the nation's capital and come home with postcards of wax saints.

Chapter 14

~

Get a Piece of the Pope

B E IT a statue or a picture, anything having to do with a
saint is guaranteed to excite a nun, but nothing is quite as
good as having the saint himself. Since there are so few saints
and you never know when another one might come along, the
Church hangs onto the ones they have for as long as possible.
Some saints have been lying in state, in glass cases like Snow
White, for hundreds of years. They don't do much anymore; not
even miracles. It only takes three postmortem miracles to
become a saint: once you've done them, why exert yourself further? You can't be promoted any higher. So they just lie there letting people see what a saint looks like.

There aren't many of them who stay presentable after long periods of time. The few that are around are mostly in cathedrals in Europe and that limits their accessibility. But saints are the celebrities of the religious world. Just as stars generate excitement in the public, saints do the same thing to nuns. People are thrilled when they see a celebrity, or touch one, or get an autograph. Nuns feel the same way about saints; only you can't get an autograph from a saint. But if you play your cards right, you can get something better than an autograph—a relic.

A relic is something that was very near and dear to a saint. It was a part of him—literally. It can be anything from a small sliver of bone to an entire finger. Our nuns had a couple of slivers. They looked like fragments of chicken bones. They kept them in small gold cases with glass tops so that we could see inside. On that saint's feast day, the nuns would drag us all over to the chapel where we would say a prayer to that saint and line up to kiss the relic.

"I can't do it," I whispered to Sister Mary Rose the first time I went through this ritual. She didn't look as though she was too crazy about it either.

"Why not?" she whispered back. I think she was hoping I had a good reason that would spare all of us.

"My mother won't let me drink out of somebody else's glass because she doesn't want me to get germs. If I catch something and she finds out that it was because I put my lips where everybody else had theirs, she'll kill me." Every now and then, Mom's rules paid off for me.

"Don't worry," she patted my shoulder as I neared the front of the line, "they tell me that gold doesn't carry germs."

Before I could think of another excuse, the gold container was right in front of my face. I kissed it fast, just barely touching the glass, and thanked God that it wasn't a whole finger.

Whose bright idea was that anyway? And where do they get

those relics? I pictured somebody like Igor hanging around the cellar of the Vatican just waiting for another canonization. There had to be a mailing department; hundreds of little boxes addressed and ready to ship that saint all over the world. And what did they do with the parts of the saint that are not particularly holy—the parts that were never allowed to be fruitful or multiply? Then you've got your big-name saints; everybody wants a piece of them. How do they satisfy those orders? Practically every church in the world has a piece of Saint Francis of Assisi. He must have been enormous.

I loved Saint Francis of Assisi as much as anybody; if he had been there in one piece, I would have been the first in line to kiss him. But that's the catch; if Saint Francis were alive and well, the nuns probably would not have allowed us to kiss him. Once somebody was dead, it was not only all right to kiss them, it was required.

Not only did we have to kiss a lot of ex-people, we also had to kiss a lot of inanimate objects. First and foremost was the bishop's ring. I would have hated to be the bishop; all those people slobbering on my hand. I'd worry about somebody snatching the ring too. I kissed the bishop's ring several times and got a good look at it. It was an expensive piece of jewelry. He didn't have just one, either. I wondered how he decided which one he would wear on any particular day. I noticed that my mother picked which jewelry she would wear according to the clothes she was wearing. I concluded that the bishop probably wore whichever ring matched his hat. That was the best thing about the bishop— he had great hats. And he wore them like Bartholomew Cubbins, one on top of another. Even the bishop's assistant, who went with him everywhere, got to wear fancy hats.

The bishop always traveled with an entourage. Along with his assistant, there were two altar boys. One altar boy walked in front of him and the other alongside. The one in front of the procession let you know that the bishop was coming before you even saw him, because of the smell. The boy carried a gold urn filled with burning incense and he swung it around in front of the bishop, for what, I don't know. If it was to fumigate the place and kill bugs, I'm sure it worked. The foul smell of that incense almost killed me a couple of times. But the bishop also brought with him a means of revival. The altar boy next to him carried a small gold pail with a gold magic wand. After the incense passed, the bishop dipped the wand in the bucket and waved it over us. It wasn't fairy dust that it sprinkled—it was holy water. Even when you were ready for it, it was a shock to be hit in the face with those icy droplets.

The things we had to go through to get in touch with God baffled me. The only reason I could see for doing them was to keep His attention by entertaining Him. The church made a great stage and had plenty of props. Everything was gold and could be handled only by a priest. The nuns were allowed to touch things like the chalice if it needed to be cleaned or moved for the priest. The rest of us could handle these things only in an emergency. When Catholic kids have a fire drill, not only are we briefed on how to get ourselves out of the building, but how to get religious articles out as well. They never went so far as to say that we should die trying to save the chalice. But they did say that the priest would. Of course, the implication was that we should be willing to give our lives too.

There was never any question in my mind as to what I would do if there was a fire. I was not going to risk my life to save any picture, statue, chalice, or even a relic. The relic is a part of a saint; but let's face it, at this point what can a fire do to him? Chances are he may have already been through one fire. That may have been how he got to heaven in the first place. I wasn't going to join him via the same route.

I felt a little guilty about that conscious decision to shirk my spiritual responsibility. Then one day, Dianne came into school with a wishbone and convinced Roseanne that it was a relic of Saint Valentino, patron saint of the movies. She proceeded to scare the wits out of Roseanne by inviting her to break it with her. Dianne promised that the winner would become a movie star. Roseanne refused to touch anybody's bones even for a chance at stardom.

I tried to convince Roseanne that Dianne was putting her on by arguing it with her logically.

"Roseanne, doesn't Dianne's relic look an awful lot like a chicken bone?"

"Sure, but so do the rest of them."

Good point. "Well, where would Dianne get a relic?"

"Her mother saved it from a burning church."

I cracked up. "Mrs. Luca!"

"She could have," Roseanne protested.

"Okay," I conceded that point. I didn't want to get into characters. "But, Roseanne, come on, patron saint of the movies?"

"Why not? They have a patron saint of everything else."

Again she was right. But I had the clincher. "If Dianne has a relic, why doesn't she show it to Sister?"

"It's a surprise. She's giving it to Sister for Christmas."

"Only if she wants to get expelled." I couldn't convince Roseanne that the chicken bone was not a relic. But then the nuns couldn't convince me that the relics were not chicken bones. I wasn't about to risk my life for them.

᠌

Chapter 15

What Do You Buy a
Nun for Christmas?

YOU WOULD think with all the religious paraphernalia
available, buying a present for a nun is a cinch. Not so.
They already have all the pictures and statues they can use, the
price of gold was a little steep, and they don't sell relics to the
general public. That left nearly every kid in the school in a panic
whenever we had to buy a present for a nun. Present-giving
came twice a year: the last day of school and Christmas. The last
day of school wasn't so bad because you knew that whatever you
gave Sister, you had an entire summer to live it down. You also
had the hope that she might be transferred and not even be
there when you got back. It was the Christmas present you had

to be careful about because you still had half a year to live with her. That put a bit of a damper on an already subdued Christmas spirit.

Long before the stores put up their Christmas displays and the radio stations started playing carols, we could feel Christmas coming. We could feel it in our bones; specifically, in our knees. We knew Christmas was coming when the prayer load got heavier. Four weeks before Christmas we broke out the Advent wreath. The Advent wreath was a wreath that lay on the table with four candles in it. The first week we lit one candle and said our prayers; the second week two candles were lit while we prayed; the third week three; and the last week, all four. It was symbolic of all the years the Jews had waited for the birth of the Savior. By the time Christmas came, I felt like I had waited as long as they had.

At about the same time the Advent prayers started, we also put up the nativity scene. Every class had one—the standard manger complete with Mary, Joseph, Jesus, Wise Men, shepherds, and barnyard animals. The second grade nativity scene had something that none of the others have, compliments of Dianne Luca. For Dianne, Christmas just wasn't Christmas without Rudolph the red-nosed reindeer. Of course, there were no reindeer in Bethlehem. So Dianne made one tiny lamb an honorary reindeer and painted his nose red. It was a few days before Sister Michael noticed the lamb's bright red nose. When she did notice it, she asked the question that all nuns do when they see something they don't like: "What is the meaning of this?" It sounded like every holy statue in the school had been desecrated.

"No one is leaving this room until one of you decides to tell me what this is all about."

I thought it was quite clear; the lamb had a red nose. The deeper meaning may have escaped her because she wasn't well versed in the Rudolph story, even though it was playing on the radio constantly. Nuns only listen to Gregorian chant stations. We sat for more than an hour in our seats with our hands folded on the desks, watching her glare, trying to sweat a confession out of us. She tried to break us by threatening to make us sit there all night until she got an answer. She didn't care if the buses left without us; she would simply call our parents to explain the problem. I had to stifle a laugh, thinking about my parents' reaction to this news.

"I'll tell you what, Sister, put the kid on the bus and I'll buy you a herd of lambs. I'll even throw in a couple of chickens."

Sitting there was a pain in the neck, but Sister wasn't anywhere near cracking me, and most of the other kids took the same attitude. Dianne sat there looking innocent. Of course, there was one person in the class who would have told the whole story before Sister even asked. The only thing that kept her silent was a fear of certain martyrdom. But at five of three, she thought that the rest of us would thank her for putting an end to this and allowing us to go home. Sandra Minelli raised her hand.

"Yes, Sandra."

"Sister, I have to go to the bathroom. Will you come with me?"

They left the room together. They weren't gone long enough to get anywhere near the bathroom. As a matter of fact, they were out of the room just long enough for Sandra to say, "Dianne Luca did it." When they came back, everybody knew what to expect. "Get your things ready to go home. We will discuss this in the morning. Dianne, you come here."

The next morning, Dianne turned in an essay about the true meaning of Christmas and the class got a lecture on that same subject from Sister. It seems that she was not a big Rudolph fan. Even Santa Claus was not high on her list. She was determined to remind us that the central theme was not "Creepy Crawlers" and other presents, but the birth of the Christ child. And so we spent the entire month of December praying to the Advent wreath or practicing for the Christmas pageant.

The Christmas pageant in an all-girl school was an experience. There is, after all, only one desirable part. And when Sandra was old enough to play it, it was hers. She was the Blessed Mother in seventh and eighth grade. The most likely place for the rest of us to end up was in the choir. The girls in the choir had to stand on bleachers for the entire hour and a half of the pageant. It got awfully hot in the spotlight that shone on them and at least one girl fainted per performance. The choir was instructed to go on singing as though nothing had happened. The girls on either side of the fainter were to move aside and let the nuns, who stood close by waiting for this to happen, take care of it. They moved in and dragged the girl off the bleachers and the song went on uninterrupted. Their favorite story about this was one about a girl who fell and hit her head on one of the pianos. She broke her glasses, she cut her face—she was a mess. But the choir went on singing with such gusto that no one even heard the thud when the poor girl touched down. The nuns took great pride in their ability to make us carry on with whatever we were doing no matter what happened around us.

Since being in the choir was a health hazard, any stage part was a privilege. You were only on for a little while and then you could sit down backstage. There was a price; aside from the Blessed Mother, there were no female parts. And, we were told, all the men of that time were bearded, which was pretty traumatic to a girl of thirteen. Since Sandra had the Blessed Mother bit tied up, the only hope for the rest of us to escape being bearded was being picked for the part of an angel. I was not angel material, but I managed to get off relatively easy by being the innkeeper. It wasn't as embarrassing as most parts because all I had to do was poke my head out the door long enough to tell

Mary and Joseph to get lost. I was believable too. I loved the idea of making Sandra Minelli sleep in a barn.

Roseanne was the one who got the worst part that last year. She was one of the wise men. The wise men were onstage for a good portion of the show. Two of them were bearded. Roseanne was not. She appeared a la Al Jolson, in black face. The nuns omitted the white around the lips, but she did have to wear white gloves. Between this, and their portrayal of pagan babies, "Amos and Andy" looked like a giant leap forward in race relations.

We all envied Sandra that Saturday night and Sunday afternoon performance. She knelt there holding the doll who was playing the baby Jesus, glowing as though she had really done it. It made us sick and apparently we weren't the only ones. On Sunday afternoon as Sandra was hamming it up with the Savior in her arms, there arose not a choir of angels, but a sudden and unexpected thud. The doll's head fell off and proceeded to roll across the stage. It came to a stop in front of a dumbfounded shepherd, who looked at it for a minute and then pushed it into the orchestra pit. Sister Michael was in the wings waving her arms hysterically. Despite Sister's prompting, the choir did not break into song. They broke into laughter. Sandra's big moment was spoiled and she was on the verge of tears. But the curtain did not come down. The show went on.

Even Sandra heaved a sigh of relief when the Christmas pageant was over. That left one last thing before Christmas vacation—the party. It was held in the gym and the whole school went. Each class was responsible for providing some refreshment. Every child brought an exchange gift for someone in their own class. Names had been drawn out of a beanie the week before. I prayed that Sandra didn't pick my name. Sandra's gift was always a pair of rosary beads or a statue. The big thrill was supposed to be that she'd had it blessed by Father Joseph. Father Joseph would bless anything, anywhere, anytime, at no cost. I was not impressed with Sandra's gifts. Since this was the one time of the year when the nuns allowed the distribution of civilian items, even a handkerchief went over better than anything religious.

We were even allowed to wear regular clothes to the party. It did begin with prayers, and we did have to sit at class tables and go up for our food by class and in a straight line; even partying was done in orderly fashion. When we finished eating we sang Christmas carols; the regular ones like "Santa Claus is Coming to Town," and "Rudolph the Red-Nosed Reindeer." Then Santa— actually Father Joseph dressed up—came to give out the presents we had laid under the Christmas tree that the nuns had put up in the corner. If you concentrated real hard, you could almost feel that glimmer of Christmas spirit that you get when you see the Christmas displays in department stores in mid-November.

I wondered what the nuns did after we left to go home and really celebrate. Most of them stayed at the convent. On Christmas morning, they probably went to mass, had breakfast, and opened the presents that we gave them, presents from their families and ones exchanged among themselves. There was nothing interesting in their Christmas packages; at least not from us children. Most of the mothers, since they were the ones who really bought the presents, stuck to the safe items like black gloves, black umbrellas, black scarves, and other black accessories. My mother, much to my chagrin, tried to be imaginative. She insisted that nuns were people too.

I think my mother actually enjoyed Christmas shopping for the nuns. She made one mistake—she dragged me along to the store with her. Her life would have been a lot easier if she'd just told me that there were black gloves in the box that I was giving to Sister. It didn't matter to me that at least five other kids in the class would be giving her gloves. That way, I wouldn't stand out in her memory. But I had to go through the agony of seeing the deviant present I was giving her. My mother's two favorite choices of presents for a nun were a nightgown or a bottle of wine. The first stop was always the lingerie department of the store where we stopped to look at seminormal nightgowns. "Are you sick!" I would scream at my mother right in the middle of the store. "Is this your idea of a joke? Do you like to see me suffer?" She was laughing. "So it is a joke! You're not the one who has to face her after she sees this! Nuns just don't wear things like this."

"How do you know that?"

"Because they are nuns. They have to wear regulation clothes. They probably have their own clothes stores where they buy their nightgowns. They'd probably get kicked out of the convent for wearing something like this."

"They would not. They do their shopping in the same stores that we do."

"Oh, really, take me to the habit department."

"Don't be wise. Now it's either this or a bottle of wine."

"What is she going to do with a bottle of wine?"

"Drink it."

"Are you sure? Have you ever seen a nun drink?"

"Of course I have. They drink wine."

"Good. Let's get the bottle of wine." I pictured this nun with a bottle of wine hidden in her drawer under all her black gloves. If I was lucky, she would get blasted on it and forget who gave it to her. I was not the least bit comfortable about giving a nun a bottle of wine for Christmas and my mother's reassurance left something to be desired.

"It's something she wouldn't buy for herself," she cajoled.

"I'll bet!"

"Oh, come on, she'll appreciate it. I promise."

I knew she was sincere in her promise, but how much could I trust her judgment? This was, after all, the woman who swore that nuns were just regular people. I had no choice in the matter, though; she was the one with the money. She bought the wine, took it home, wrapped it up, and sent me off to school with it. It must have been an all right gift because I never heard about it later. Selecting a gift for a nun that wouldn't get you thrown out of school was a traumatic experience. It was the one thing that made kids grateful that Christmas came only once a year.

Chapter 16

What Did You
Give Up for Lent?

THE CHRISTMAS prayer season lasted well into January.
That gave us February with just the regular prayers. But
then in March began the heaviest prayer season of the year:
Lent. Lent is the penitent season; after a year of what would
hardly be described as utter abandon, it needs to be approached
with a sense of humor. I found Ash Wednesday rather helpful to
that end. We all got dragged over to the chapel so that Father
could bless us and make the sign of the cross on our foreheads
with ashes. I had bangs at the time, so I would hold them back
while Father applied my ashes. When he was through I let the
bangs fall back into place and I looked perfectly normal. The

nuns did not. They spent the whole day with dirty foreheads.

If the purpose of putting ashes on people's heads was to make us all spend the day thinking about the Church, it worked. On Ash Wednesday, the first day of Lent, I couldn't concentrate on my schoolwork; not when my teacher had a dirty forehead. I was also painfully conscious of the ashes on my own forehead. I could still feel Father's thumb pressing against my skin, making the sign of the cross. It was as though something was trying to penetrate my skull. Sister said that it was the Holy Spirit. But I didn't feel the least bit holy.

My understanding of this ritual was that the ashes were a symbol of penitence. They were the mark of a sinner trying to make retribution. I was not as comfortable being a sinner as some people were. The nuns, for example, wore their ashes proudly; proclaiming to the world that they were sinners. This confused me since they spent the rest of the year touting their spotless lifestyle. Were they doing things that they weren't letting us in on? Or did they just fantasize on Ash Wednesday about all the things they would have liked to have done to earn those ashes?

But Ash Wednesday was only the beginning of weeks of double-duty penance. Once we'd been besmirched with the ashes, the next order of business was for Sister to find out what we'd given up for Lent. It was not enough to admit to our frailty; we had to do something to make restitution to God. The nuns told us that the best way to do this was to punish ourselves by forfeiting, for Lent's entire duration, one of our greatest pleasures. They would help us by keeping track of our lenten resolutions and keeping an eye on us to see that we stuck to them. That was why it was always safer to give up something that was done at home, preferably in private. That way all they could do was ask periodically if you were keeping to it. They never told us what they gave up. That was a matter between them and God, they would say whenever we asked, and they were old enough not to need help.

I gave up candy one year for Lent and from Ash Wednesday to Easter Sunday, I did not touch candy. During that time I went heavy on cakes, pies, ice cream, and cookies, but not one bite of candy. It wasn't Sister's watching me that kept me to it. I'd made a bargain with God and I didn't want to break my word. I was proud of myself for sticking to my word, but at the same time, I realized how silly it was to trouble God with my eating habits. Depriving oneself of small pleasures doesn't do any good for anybody. From then on, I decided during Lent that I would try to be extra conscious about being a good person. Nonetheless I had to tell Sister what I was giving up. Just trying to be a good person wouldn't make the grade. I wanted to get some ideas about what sorts of things adults gave up so that I could give her a mature answer. I asked my father.

"Well, I had a hard time trying to decide what I should give up for Lent," he told me seriously. "It was between skydiving and alligator wrestling."

I was exasperated. I had trouble enough trying to understand why I was supposed to do what the nuns told us to do without my own father being flip about it. I looked at his face. He was watching me, smiling. In his own peculiar way, he was telling me something serious. "So which one did you give up?"

"Skydiving."

I laughed and he put his arm around me.

"Yeah, I like alligator wrestling too much."

"I think I'll give up school. It won't be easy. But if you help me, I think I can stick to it."

What I really gave up that last year was giving up things for Lent. The nuns gave us so much penance we didn't need to impose more upon ourselves. During Lent we did not say the rosary. That was a relief; but we'd learned long ago that the only time you got relief in Catholic school was when something worse was to follow. We were excused from the rosary every day to say the stations of the cross instead. That was done in the chapel. It was also done, for the most part, on our knees. During the agony of the stations of the cross—ours, not Christ's—I longed for the good old days of sitting in the classroom with my hands folded on my desk, saying the rosary.

There are fourteen stations. A picture of each was on the walls of the chapel; seven up one wall and seven down the opposite wall. Upon entering the chapel, we were all handed little booklets with the special prayers in them and then Sister ushered us into our pews. The girl who was leading the prayers began at the back of the chapel, in front of the first station. She knelt down and read the prayer. This took forever because the prayers were not only unfamiliar but were written in language even my father had trouble reading. It was English; but none of us understood a word of it. After we responded to the first prayer, the leader got up and went to the second station and knelt down in front of it. She did this fourteen times and it took just over forty-five minutes. While the leader of the prayers had the relief of standing up for a second between prayers, the rest of us remained kneeling the entire time. We stood only after the fourteenth station to finish the prayers.

There is a trick to being able to kneel that long to Sister's liking. After about five minutes, your back started to ache and after ten, your knees got numb. If you made any obvious movements to alleviate your discomfort, Sister (who was always watching) would poke you in the small of the back. That was particularly deadly if you had to go to the bathroom, which was often the case toward the end. What you had to do was learn to move only the hips, which were well concealed under those pleated wool skirts. You could move your hips forward a few inches, arching your back and stretching those sore muscles. Then move your hips back, arching the other way. This gave some relief for a minute or two. Then you work on the knees. You move your weight onto one knee and jiggle the other one slightly to get the blood moving again. Then do the same with the other knee.

Instead of a room full of kids trying to break the fifteen-minute rosary without getting caught, we had a room full of kids trying to alleviate their pain without getting caught. It was like martyr practice. Once we'd said the stations of the cross we could really appreciate, firsthand, the suffering they depicted.

We suffered "the way of the cross" for what seemed like an eternity. Finally, we came into the home stretch: Palm Sunday. Palm Sunday is the only Sunday of the year that children are actually anxious to go to church. Kids try to get there early so that they can get the front seats and get a good share of those palm leaves.

I'm certain that it was because of kids like Pauli that the palms weren't distributed until near the end of the mass. Somewhere along the line, Pauli got the idea that the palms were a kind of a weapon. It was a natural mistake for somebody with Pauli's intellectual capacities, since so much about the Church centers around violence. On Palm Sunday, Pauli declared church a combat zone. He could pick somebody off two rows away with one of those palm leaves. But he overestimated his prowess. He swiped at the little pink flowers on Lena's Easter bonnet one time too many. When she'd had enough, she turned around and beat him under the pew with her own palms. She handled them better than her broom. Pauli had chosen the wrong person for palm-to-palm combat. After mass, he repaired the damage done to his ego. Using guerrilla tactics, he swooped down on an unsuspecting altar boy, reestablishing his dominance.

Palm Sunday was almost more exciting than Easter. It meant that we only had to say the stations of the cross three more times. We didn't have school on Holy Thursday or Good Friday. We were supposed to be too busy praying to be able to do any work. On Good Friday, between the hours of noon and three, the time that Christ was supposed to have been on the cross, we were supposed to meditate. During that time we were to be completely silent: no work, no play, no television or radio, no reading unless it was prayers. We were also supposed to fast all day. At my house on Good Friday I always felt like I was living in Sodom or Gommorah because everything went on as usual. Only the older people were somewhat subdued; but then, they always were.

On Saturday all the women were cooking and baking for Easter. We dyed Easter eggs and got out our fancy clothes for the next day. The main concerns on Easter Sunday were the Easter baskets full of candy, the Easter egg hunt in the park, seeing everybody's new clothes, and eating. Everybody went to church, even the people who hadn't been since Christmas. The early masses were SRO, because everybody wanted to get it over with so that they could enjoy the holiday. The church was bright and full of flowers. The statues, which had been covered with purple cloth during Lent, were uncovered again. And the priest was no longer dressed in purple, but in white. Unfortunately, because he was playing to a packed house, he gave the longest sermon of the year. During the entire thing, Pauli was throwing jelly beans and other kids were trying to catch them to eat them. Inevitably one would land in some nun's lap and she would calmly pick it up and put it into her pocket. Later that day, while I was eating the ears off my big chocolate bunny, devouring marshmallow chicks, popping one chocolate egg after another, and digging through the plastic grass in the basket to make sure I wasn't missing anything, I was sure Sister was off savoring her jelly bean.

Chapter 17

~

The May Crowning

THE YEAR was coming quickly to a close—at least that was what my mother tried to convince me. For me, time wasn't passing nearly fast enough and it surely didn't pass fast enough for the nuns not to be able to sneak in another reason for special prayers. As all of us who went to Catholic school, or even catechism, know, May is the month of Mary. On the very first school day in May every class built a shrine to the Statue of the Blessed Mother. We set the statue on a table in the corner of the room. Sister brought material to cover the table and to drape down from the wall behind the statue. We put a vase on either side of the statue and every day in May two girls were responsible for bringing fresh flowers.

Every morning, Sandra made her grandstand show of paying homage to the statue. Before she went to her seat she would go over to the statue and kneel down in front of it and move her lips in silent prayer. I was sure that the reason she was so crazy about statues of the Blessed Mother was because her mother had deprived her of Barbie dolls in her formative years. Whether it was her turn or not, Sandra brought flowers for the Blessed Mother every day. The nuns were impressed with her love and devotion. She said her rosary with extra zeal that month, which meant extra slowly.

Not only were we saying the rosary every day, we were also singing songs. Sister would toot her little pitch pipe and we would all begin on a different note, half-humming because we didn't know the words. All the while, Sister would be waving her arms to try to make us sing louder. Sandra carried the show and Sister would always compliment her on that. If she'd asked us to do "Hey Jude," she would have seen the enthusiasm she was looking for. But we weren't doing popular rock numbers, we were doing Blessed Mother numbers and we'd been practicing them since just after Easter.

This time the show was the May Crowning. It took place on the first Sunday afternoon in May and all our parents and friends of the school came. We wore the pink gowns we had to buy along with our uniforms for special occasions like this. We all lined up single file outside the gym, from kindergarten to twelfth grade. A few girls had special honors. Some of the smaller children carried baskets of flower petals, which they scattered along the parade route. This little job had its disadvantage—bees. It was not an unusual sight in the May parade to see a small girl lose the flower petals in one lump trying to swat the bees with the basket. Then she would get a look of disapproval from whichever nun was closest to her. They walked alongside the procession, spaced every few yards to make sure we were singing, praying, and staying in an absolutely straight line.

At the very back of the procession was Father Joseph, carrying his incense. He was accompanied by two kindergartners dressed up as angels and two altar boys that we had bused in from another Catholic school since we had no boys of our own. Just in front of them was the one girl who had been singled out for the highest honor of the year; the one who would crown the Blessed Mother with a garland of flowers.

We marched around the grounds for what seemed like hours, singing and praying all the while, with the parents gathering along the procession route to take pictures. Finally we ended up in front of the statue of the Blessed Mother. It was a life-size statue on an ivy-covered pedestal. There we knelt on the grass and prayed interminably. Finally we got to the big number, "O Mary We Crown Thee with Blossoms Today." As we sang, the crowner took her garland of flowers and mounted the stairs behind the statue to the pedestal. When she got to the top, she held the wreath above the statue's head. On the last note of the song, she placed the flowers, ever so reverently, on the statue's head. She came down, we said a few more prayers, and it was done.

That one statue got more attention than any of the people at that school, not to mention respect. During the May Crowning I couldn't help thinking about the first commandment, and God's feelings about worshipping false idols. The key word here is "false." Worshipping the real thing seemed to be just fine. Every year the nuns bought flowers for that statue; I can't remember their ever doing that for a human being. I couldn't help wondering why we made such a big deal over a statue.

It wasn't that I objected to paying respect to Mary. She was the mother of Jesus Christ and that wasn't an easy job, but she did it well. She was a great woman, one deserving of respect. She could have been a terrific role model if only the nuns had allowed us to identify with her. But they kept her superhuman and made her big selling point the fact that she was the Virgin Mother. That concept gave me trouble from the very beginning. They told us that she was pregnant before she had a husband. So at first, I thought that unwed motherhood was a sure sign of purity. It emulated the Blessed Mother. Then I learned about the specifics of conception and the nuns told us that hers was immaculate, she was untouched. But there was a girl in the neighborhood who was pregnant and claiming the same thing and nobody was promoting her for sainthood.

Then I thought about my own mother and my own conception. I did not like the idea of being unimmaculate. Though I understood and believed that Jesus Christ was special, I could not accept that the rest of us were somehow tarnished from the very beginning. There is only one way to make babies and it's the way God set it up. To say Mary didn't do it that way and was, as a result, immaculate, seems to be critical of God's system.

They never did tell us exactly whether Mary was a wife to Joseph in the biblical sense after she gave birth to Jesus. I always felt sorry for Saint Joseph and thought he deserved his sainthood if only for the fact that he was the most highly underrated person in the Church. The nuns rarely talked about Joseph, except to say what a saintly man he was for having a son whom he could not take for his own and a wife whom he could not take for his own. And he died young—no wonder!

They all died young, except for Mary. She didn't die at all. She ascended. When God thought that the time was right, He brought her right up to heaven, body and all. According to the nuns, this woman did only one human thing and that was suffer through the deaths of her husband and her son. And at the same time they were holding her up as an example for all women, particularly mothers, to follow. On Mothers Day, still the month of Mary, the young children colored pictures of Mary and pasted them on hearts for their mothers; the rest of us were usually rail-roaded into buying little statues of her. The nuns assured us that this was the perfect present for our mothers. Mine usually ended up in a cabinet down in the cellar. That was all right, though, because I always bought her a real present too. The only reason I gave her the statue at all was to give her a taste of what I had to go through every day.

I think my mother had trouble relating to the Blessed Mother. I certainly did. They told us that she was thirteen years old when she had Jesus—just our age. We should have been able to understand her, empathize with her, but we just couldn't. She was a mother and that was something none of us had even con-sidered. The only thing we had in common with her was virgin-ity. And none of us, except Sandra, planned to go professional with that. We were all what the nuns called "boy crazy." After nine years of Catholic school, we were just plain crazy. Even Pauli was looking good. He had a Beatles haircut, peach fuzz, and pagan morals; the same morals that the rest of us harbored secretly.

None of us were looking to become fallen women, but we all agreed that virginity as a lifelong practice was highly overrated. All the women in my family tried it and must not have liked it, because sooner or later they all quit. The only women I knew who did stick with it were the nuns; that was probably what made them so grouchy. To preserve my personality, I figured that some year I would just give it up for Lent.

Chapter 18

≈

Sister Was Not Impressed When She Found Me Reading *The Confessions of Saint Augustine*

WITH JUST a few weeks of school to go, our class suddenly became very special. We were preparing for our eighth grade graduation ceremony. We practiced walking from the convent to the pagoda where the ceremony would take place. We practiced the songs we would sing, the grand finale being, "When You Walk Through a Storm"—something we felt we'd been doing for nine years. We practiced sitting and standing at the appropriate times. And we listened to the valedictory speech by guess who at least half a million times, ingesting more saccharin from Sandra's voice than has ever been given to any laboratory rat. Very early on in all this practicing, we had to go out and buy graduation gowns and shoes. We didn't wear the standard cap and gown. I suppose that was our reprieve after nine years of uniforms; to be able to look different from one another on our way out. There were requirements, though. The gowns had to have long sleeves (in June) and a high neckline. They had to be ankle length and pure white. We were going to look like vestal virgins fleeing the temple.

Three weeks before graduation we had to bring our gowns and shoes into school for Sister to approve them. She wasn't about to trust us after the fashion battle we'd had just a few months before. Sister knew that whenever we were off school grounds, we would roll our skirts up. She could tell how boy crazy a girl was by the number of horizontal wrinkles there were under the waistband of the skirt. She also knew that the problem with rolling the skirt up was that after you rolled it even twice, you looked like you were wearing an inner tube around your middle. And that was why she was mortified with the arrival of "beer jackets." The baggy white jackets were not only stylish, but almost long enough to hide the uniform completely. And, to add insult to injury, they were also a means of artistic self-expression. We decorated them with indelible markers. Mine had a "Ban the Bomb" symbol on the pocket, said "sock it to me" on the back, and had little footprints and other artwork and Sixties sayings all over.

The nuns hated the jackets so adamantly that one day they issued a statement saying that we were not allowed to wear them to school. Dianne Luca saved us. "Sister, this is the only jacket I own. My mother cannot afford to go out and buy me another one just to suit your taste." Dianne Luca, the kid with two dozen pairs of shoes.

"Maybe we should just ask your mothers how they feel about these jackets of yours."

"Why don't you do that?" we called their bluff. We were all

sure that our mothers would be behind us on this one. We were teenage girls. They were afraid to defy us. The jackets stayed. And it was because of that that Sister took great pleasure in inspecting our graduation gowns. She would not lose another round to us. Though each one of us suffered Sister's careful scrutiny, only Dianne's gown failed inspection. It had a high neck in front, but the back plunged to her waist. She brought it back to the store and exchanged it for another which also failed inspection. The nuns thought that it was too lacy and transparent, and the fact that she would be wearing a slip under it didn't sway their opinion. Dianne got a third gown which finally passed. Sandra had by far the most dazzling gown. She looked like a Southern belle fresh off the plantation, with her long blond hair all tied up in ribbons just like the first day I met her. Her shoes had heels high enough to ensure her being the last in line once again.

Sandra would be the star of this performance in every way. But we were all used to that by now and it couldn't possibly put a damper on our enthusiasm about graduating. More than half of us would be going on to different high schools; our parents realized we'd done our penance. We were anxious to get out into that impious world of civilian clothes and boys. The thought of not having to say the rosary every day, or kneel for hours on special occasions, seemed like a mirage in a desert. We couldn't believe it could be true, but we went rushing toward it anyway. The nuns realized this; as a going away present, they gave us one last guilt trip for the road.

"We have spent all these years investing in your souls. We devote our lives to this mission. Some of you will be leaving us soon." She didn't mention names. She didn't have to; we were the ones who were smiling. "It will probably be good for you to experience other methods of teaching as long as you keep with you the strong foundation that we have built here and spread your faith to others. Most of the people you meet will not have been privileged to have had your religious background. Some, rather than accepting your knowledge, will try to convince you to behave according to their lower standards. Theirs will be an easier way of life than we have trained you to accept. We will pray that you do not give in to these temptations. May God's grace go with you."

Feeling somewhat sentimental, only because I knew that I would soon be free, I wanted to show the nuns that their time had not been completely wasted on me. Some of the things they had taught me did sink in. I did want to be a good person. I had tried for years to impress that upon them by "just being myself," to no avail. So, for those last few weeks of school, I tried to act like Sandra Minelli. My mouth said the rosary zealously, even though I couldn't force my mind to pay attention. I stopped wearing my beer jacket—it was too hot anyway. I didn't throw away food; I bought only fruit on the pretense that I was on a diet. And I tried to ask religious questions to show the nuns that I was interested in acquiring knowledge about the Church.

Sister Mary Rose suggested I find a book that told the story of a saint. I thought that was a pretty good idea. I would kill two birds with one stone: I would have a good read and impress the nuns at the same time. I went to the school library; the large selection of books about saints covered almost an entire wall. It was impossible to judge these books by their covers. They were all titled *The Story of Saint* somebody or other. There was no way of telling what sort of story it would be. I had only one requirement: no martyr stuff. I'd had enough of those gory details to last me a lifetime. One caught my eye, *The Confessions of Saint Augustine*. It sounded perfect for me. I figured that at least it would give me some idea of what sorts of confessions to make up when I hadn't committed any good sins. I was the first one to take it out; it must have been newly donated. That was how our library got all its books.

I didn't start reading right away, but I carried the book with me everywhere I went, hoping the nuns would see the effort I was making. I was disappointed when none of them acknowledged the book in my hand. They always took note of which religious book Sandra was reading. I decided that they didn't notice because they took it for granted that I didn't read that sort of material. I had to do something to draw their attention to the title of the book. One day, before the bell rang, I was waiting in front of the school when Sister Michael happened by. I took the opportunity and dropped my books. I made a big production of picking them up. She couldn't help but notice.

"Now you see why we want you to put covers on your books." She took the opportunity to make a point of her own. "Accidents like this happen and if the books aren't covered, they might be damaged."

"Yes, Sister." I smiled up at her, picking up the library book and brushing it off with special care.

"What is that?"

"It's my library book," I answered, pleased that she had seen it and commented on it. I was expecting some of the approval that up until now was reserved for Sandra.

"Let me see that."

I handed over the book, enjoying the look of surprise on her face.

"Where did you get this?"

"At the library."

"Our library?"

"Yes, Sister." I was getting much more attention than Sandra ever did.

"Well, there must have been some mistake."

She was more surprised than I thought she would be. "No, Sister, it's no mistake. This is the one I wanted to read."

"No doubt," she muttered. "This book does not belong in our

library. It is above your level of comprehension. I'll take it and straighten it out with the librarian." She turned and headed for the library.

I was left standing there, wondering what that conversation had meant. Since that was how almost all my conversations with the nuns left me, I should have just shrugged it off. I hadn't realized before that some saints are more saintly than others. And of all the saints in the library, I had to pick a dud! This guy was so bad that he was getting thrown out of our library. It occurred to me that once again I was interested in all the wrong things. It wasn't the *confessions* of Saint Augustine in which they wanted us to be interested; it was the good works he performed after he reformed.

We were supposed to be interested in prayer and sacrifice and the nuns thought if we read about the prayers and sacrifices of others, it would inspire us to emulate them. I'd been in Catholic school long enough to feel as though if you've heard one prayer, you've heard them all. Books about people spending hours upon hours on their knees could not hold my interest. I liked more action-packed stories. The more I thought about it, the more I felt that those confessions of Saint Augustine must have been pretty interesting for Sister to have taken them away from me. She said I wouldn't be able to comprehend the book. She wished that were true. I could comprehend sins just fine; it was miracles I had trouble with.

Those nuns loved to protect us from knowledge of regular human life. They guarded us from things that would subvert our impressionable minds—like history. Oh, we studied history. We knew how many missions there were in Africa and when they were established. We knew what the Roman Empire did to the Christians, what happened to Joan of Arc, and all about Henry VIII while he was "the protector of the faith" and the pope's good buddy. We were well versed in history; except the "heathen" accounts thereof. The nuns told us that there would be time enough to learn about the pagan's view of the progression of the world after we had a clear picture of how it really happened.

They advised those of us who were leaving that since our education was far from complete we should seek out religious instruction in addition to our academic studies. I thought about it every time I wanted a good laugh. I'd been going to Catholic school for nine years, every day under protest. The last thing in the world I would do was volunteer for more, no matter how clouded my mind was with the euphoria of being sprung. Once I marched off that pagoda in step with "Pomp and Circumstance" with my diploma in hand and got safely behind the bushes near the convent that marked the end of the procession—that was the end.

The big day finally came after a week of scrubbing the classroom. We had cleaned meticulously. Even the books were clean. Sister watched us go through them, page by page, and erase all pencil marks. We also cleaned the edges of the pages. We did it by closing the book and then rubbing the pages with sandpaper until they were white again. I wondered if the books got smaller and smaller after every cleaning. But all that was forgotten when we marched away from the convent in time with the music. All our parents were there, seated alphabetically. I caught sight of Mrs. Luca in her brightly colored, flowered minidress. She was wearing wire-rimmed pink sunglasses. Standing next to her was one of Dianne's notorious "uncles" who, we'd figured out years before, was not really related.

I looked over at my parents as I passed them, despite the orders not to do that. My mother was crying. My mother would cry at supermarket openings. I had known she would cry and had warned her not to embarrass me that way. When I looked at her, she put her sunglasses on. I suppose she had a legitimate reason to cry. Her little girl had grown up despite the odds against survival in that environment. Her first words to me after the ceremony were, "Now, wasn't it really worth all that complaining?"

Caught up in all the excitement of the day, in the midst of all the parents hugging and kissing their daughters, I smiled and put my arms around my mother and told her exactly what she wanted to hear: "Absolutely."

≈

Chapter 19

The Pink Slip
from the Rome Office

I NEVER THOUGHT that it would really happen, but I was
out. It was a somewhat honorable discharge too. Some people weren't so lucky. You could be thrown out in disgrace at any
time, even after you were dead. That happened to one guy who
was almost sainted. During the final hearings for sainthood, it is
customary that the body of the candidate be exhumed. On this
occasion, the person who would otherwise have been sainted
was rejected because of the position of his body. The body was in
a position of despair; that is, face frozen in mid-scream, fists
clenched, body twisted. Obviously, the person had been buried

alive, woke up, found out where he was, and lost his composure and his sainthood.

I do understand that the Church requires a certain amount of decorum, especially from its higher-ups. But I do think that there are times when certain allowances can be made and reactions to severe circumstances can be overlooked. I think that being buried alive qualifies as one of these circumstances. If you want to blame somebody, blame the idiot who buried him. What on earth did they expect him to do, say the rosary? Is that why they pack them with you when you go?

The Church has its standards and sees to it that all followers live up to those standards. If not, they are out. No one escapes this scrutiny; not saints, not even nuns. Because Mother Superior decided that she was not suited to convent life, Sister Mary Rose was asked to leave.

Two years after I graduated from eighth grade, I was walking through a department store and I saw somebody who looked familiar, but not quite. I stared for a while until she caught me staring and started walking toward me.

"Hello," she said, "how have you been?"

I kept staring, actually I think I was gawking at that point, my mind racing for a name. Then it dawned on me. "Sister?" I said sheepishly.

She smiled; that wide grin that used to cross her face every time she fixed something just right. "Not anymore. Just Mary now."

"Oh." I was dumbfounded, as though she'd just told me that somebody had died. "Well, how are you?" I stumbled over my words. I couldn't believe that she'd left the convent.

"Fine, thank you."

"You look really great," I said too enthusiastically. She had hair. It was long and dark and curled. She was wearing a real dress; a minidress. And she had legs; real legs all the way up to the thighs. I felt as though I had witnessed the transformation of Pinocchio into a real boy. I caught myself acting like a jerk.

"Thank you," she answered, smiling at my innocent clumsiness. "You look very well too."

"Thanks."

"How are you doing in school?"

"Fine. I like it a lot." I wished I could have told her what it was like for me those first few months. I was overwhelmed by the freedom, even uncomfortable with it. In my new school, we didn't have to raise our hands to go to the bathroom. During free periods, we could go to the student center or the snack bar or even outside. And when we took tests, the teacher left the room; he said we were on the honor system. During my first few months I spent all my free time in the library. That was the only place I felt as though I belonged because it was the only place that had rules. But I got over that. "I'm doing fine in school." My lack of eloquence was torturous. "Are you still teaching?"

"I did for a while, but now I'm being a housewife."

Married! I checked the finger. The crucifix was gone, replaced by a plain gold band. "That's nice. Congratulations."

She smiled and nodded.

"Well, I have to be going now. It was nice to see you."

"It was nice seeing you too," she answered.

I walked away, relieved that I didn't have to embarrass myself anymore. For so many years, I had seen her every day, had talked to her every day, but as a nun. I didn't know how to talk to her as a person. I wish I had. She was always a nice nun and she seemed like a nice person too. Shocked as I was about seeing her, I couldn't help feeling happy that she was out.

One other person got out that year—Dianne Luca. She was asked to leave St. Lucy's High School. It seems that Dianne's favorite subject was biology, specifically male anatomy. During a spring dance at the high school, one of the nuns caught her doing heavy experimentation in an empty classroom. The nun dragged her to the office after dismissing Dianne's specimen and began lecturing her on morality. During this lecture, the nun was punctuating her points by poking at Dianne with her finger. Each time the nun poked her, Dianne backed away from her. The nun kept advancing until she poked Dianne and she fell backward over a chair. She flipped right over and landed on her back. Immediately she began screaming, "My back, my back. You broke it. I'm crippled. I can't move."

The nun ran out of the room to get help. When she left the room, Dianne started rolling around the floor, laughing. It would have worked out just fine if Dianne hadn't been so amused by her performance. When the nun came back with two other panic-stricken nuns, they found Dianne still rolling with laughter. The next day, a letter was drafted to Dianne's mother telling her that out of the goodness of their hearts, the nuns would allow Dianne to finish out the last few weeks of school there. They did not, however, feel that they could allow her to return the following year. Dianne, they said, was a disruptive influence and though they were concerned with her spiritual well-being, they also had a responsibility to all the other girls. They sent their regrets. Dianne had no regrets. She'd been trying to get out for eleven years. Her only regret was that they'd only kicked her out of the school and not the whole Church. But just as eligibility for sainthood requires extreme qualifications, the opposite is true as well. To be eligible for excommunication a person has to be able to drive even Saint Jude, patron saint of impossible causes, to the brink of despair. Dianne was close, but no cigar.

Excommunication is something that is discussed in the same ominous, hushed tones that people used to use when talking about unwed motherhood. But getting excommunicated is much worse than getting pregnant; pregnant, they can forgive, after proper penance. Excommunication is the final word. It comes right from the top too; not God, but the pope. No one ever told us what the actual procedure for excommunication was. God willing, it was something that we would never have to know. But I wondered about it. How did the pope know that you were committing an excommunicable offense? And once he found out, did he fly you to Rome and stand you up in front of a crowd in Saint Peter's Square for a holy court-martial in which he ripped off your scapular and broke your rosary beads? Maybe he just sent a singing telegram—Gregorian chant, of course. It might be worth getting excommunicated just to find out how it's done. But the one thing they did not teach us about the Church was how to get out of it.

They tried to scare us by telling us that if you get thrown out that's it. You will be denied your privileges as a Catholic for the rest of your life. Privileges?! Once excommunicated, a person cannot go to church ever again. That didn't scare me because I'd already stopped going, unless there was a wedding or a funeral.

Chapter 20

≈

The Pilgrimage

WHEN I finally went to church, I went to *church*—Saint Peter's Basilica, Rome. It was the summer after I graduated from high school. I was all grown up; and so were my parents. They were less affected by things that used to embarrass them to tears, like their children's behavior, particularly in public places where we knew we had them at a disadvantage.

But it was I, not they, who was embarrassed in the Vatican. My youngest sister, who was eleven and still going to school at Saint Lucy's, was busy looking for things to photograph that would impress the nuns. She found something very early on.

"Come here," she called to me.

"What is it?"

"What's that?" she whispered, pointing to a pope lying in state.

"It's a pope." I started walking away.

She grabbed me by the arm. "Wait a minute. You mean a statue of a pope?"

"No. A real pope."

"A dead one?"

"Well, they don't come in here to take a nap in that glass case. Of course, a dead one."

"How long's he been there?"

"Couple of hundred years, I guess."

"Dead?"

"Dead."

"A dead pope?" she said in a faint voice, nodding toward him again.

I nodded yes.

"Oh, my God." Her voice was getting a little louder. "A dead pope." Louder still. "That's sick," she shrieked. Her voice reverberated off the walls of the Basilica.

"Shhh." I tried to quiet her, but instead brought more attention to the two of us.

"A dead pope," she repeated. "I can't believe it. That is really sick." She put her camera to her eye and started clicking pictures, all the while commenting how sick it was.

I looked around for my parents, the same parents who had dragged me out of the parish church for singing. They were casually ambling around, looking over their shoulders at us like, "Whose kids are those?"

Luckily the nuns at Saint Lucy's didn't witness the scene. But they would have been thrilled to see those pictures of the pope. Undoubtedly they would pass them around the classroom and expect every child to marvel at the sight of a dead pope.

Those pictures would be concrete proof of everything they had promised the Vatican would be: tomb after tomb after tomb, a monument to martyrdom.

Of course there wouldn't be time to show the kids the pictures of the brightly colored mosaics, the beauty of Michelangelo's frescoes in the Sistine Chapel, or the magnificence of Bernini's canopy. There was no way to keep eyes downcast in the Vatican, nor any way to feel humble. The splendor demanded not only attention, but also communion. Here, in the church of churches, was man's greatest tribute to God; not subjugation, but the glory of achievement. And here, being human was not something to apologize for, but something to be proud of.

To say that I was moved is a gross understatement. I felt the presence of God more profoundly than ever before. And I knew that if He was ever to propose to me, it would be there and then. But the proposal didn't come until years later.

≈

Chapter 21

"Don't Forget to Say a Prayer for Me!"

T HE PROPOSAL didn't come from God. It came from Pauli. And I decided that I was more suited to an earthly marriage—I wouldn't presume to call it a more normal marriage, since Pauli was still far from normal. He still wears sneakers with his jacket and tie and still eats as indiscriminately as a garbage disposal. And every now and then, I still have to smack him on the head.

But I have always envied him his freedom from the inhibitions and guilt that have plagued me. I was sure that my feelings were a bequest from the nuns. Even though Pauli did spend a few years in Catholic school, I thought that he'd left before it had any real impact on him. I was wrong.

One night, shortly after our daughter's first birthday, we were sitting together quietly, drinking some wine and listening to music. Out of the blue and in a somewhat alarmed voice he said, "You know, we never got the baby baptized."

"Yeah, so?"

"Well, don't you think we should?"

"Why?"

"Because we're baptized Catholics."

"Oh, do you want to raise her Catholic?" I was a little confused. If this was something that was important to him, I wondered why it had taken him this long to bring it up. Was this the same guy who was practically ready to draw up a marriage contract over what breed of dog we would have?

"I don't know," he answered.

Now I was really confused. "Well, if we get her baptized, are you going to bring her to church on Sundays?"

"No. You are."

"No. I'm not. And if you don't want to bring her to church, why do you want to get her baptized in the first place?"

"Because I don't want her to end up in limbo. I want her to come to heaven with us."

"Oh, really, do you want to tell me just who confirmed your reservations?"

"Don't worry about it." He gave me a dirty look. "I'm going to heaven."

"And so is your daughter. Do you really think that God could love her any less because nobody threw water on her?"

"Don't be stupid, of course I don't think that. Now will you get serious? Don't you think we should get her baptized?"

"Are you going to go find a priest to do it?"

"No. You are."

"No. I'm not."

"Come on, it can't hurt. And we might as well play it safe."

"All right, I'll think about it, okay?" I knew he'd forget about it for at least another year.

"Okay," he agreed and the subject was dropped.

The next day, when I came home from running a few errands, I was surprised to find the house empty. I didn't bother to look for a note; Pauli doesn't leave them, which is just as well. I'm better off not knowing what he might be up to. So it was a while before I went into the kitchen and saw, lying in plain view on the counter, a five-dollar bill. I hoped that this was his idea of a joke and not a serious message. I did hope that he wasn't off somewhere trying to find someone to baptize my pagan baby.

The five dollars turned out to be for the paper boy. But I was still left there thinking it all over again. She was better off being a pagan baby than buying them, I told myself. I couldn't imagine sending a child of mine to Saint Lucy's to be baffled by explanations of dogma and terrified by Sister Michael and stories of martyrdom. I would tell my daughter about God myself, the way He seemed to me in the arms of the gentle man in the Levi's and the flannel shirt, whose blessing to us was, "May God love you and keep you, and don't forget to say a prayer for me."

Of all the experiences I had there, all the things that are etched in my memory, that will always be the first.

About the Author

GINA CASCONE was born and raised in central New Jersey. *Pagan Babies* (1982) was her first book, soon followed by *Mother's Little Helper* (1984). In 1985, she began writing with her sister Annette under the pseudonym A. G. Cascone. The team produced more than twenty humor books, teen thrillers, and humorous spine tinglers for middle-grade readers. From 1989 to 1995, Gina and her husband owned Wit and Wisdom Booksellers, and independent bookstore in Lawrenceville, New Jersey. The mother of two children, Gina lives with her husband in New York City.

ATRIA BOOKS
PROUDLY PRESENTS

LIFE AL DENTE
Laughter and Love in an
Italian-American Family

GINA CASCONE

Atria Books Hardcover
July 2003

Turn the page for a preview of
Life al Dente. . . .

Chapter 1

~

One of the Boys

I WAS THE firstborn, the son my father always
wanted. And so he started almost immediately to
mold me into his own image and likeness. For the most
part, his efforts were successful. Unfortunately, there
was one obstacle, which he could neither overcome nor
accept. I was a girl.

My father's first words to my mother after visiting
the nursery shortly after my birth were, "It looks like a
monkey." Who was he kidding? If I'd had a blue blanket
wrapped around me, I could have been a monkey and he

would have been too delirious with joy to have noticed.

Still, son or not, I was his kid. "I guess we'll keep it," he nobly announced to my mother after the next visit.

Having thus committed himself, my father tried as hard as he could to protect me from the ugly truth of my genetic makeup for as long as he could. Maybe he even managed to convince himself that it wasn't so. Parents do tend to be blind to their children's short-comings. And in an Italian family, few things are a greater handicap than being born female.

In the early years, I didn't suffer from it at all. My father worked double-time to turn me into a real man. He taught me not to cry, "like a girl"; throw a ball under-hand, "like a sissy"; or slap—"if you're going to hit some-body, you punch him." I learned that the secret of win-ning an argument was turning up the volume of your voice and gesticulating furiously. And I learned to say *vaffanculo* when I was angry.

My mother stood by and let my father have his way as far as my upbringing was concerned. There were two reasons for this. First of all, my mother always let my father have his way. He was her most spoiled child. And secondly, she agreed with him. She wanted me to be strong, quick, and competitive—not the son she always wanted, but the daughter she always wanted.

But sooner or later the horrible truth had to catch up with me and have a real impact on my life. Neither of my parents prepared me for that day. I suppose they meant to and just kept putting it off until it was too late.

It certainly would have been easier hearing it from them than from Little Nicky Santucci.

Little Nicky ran the neighborhood—insofar as all activities regarding us kids were concerned. He was, for all intents and purposes the self-proclaimed mayor of Melrose Avenue. It was a tight, little street. The houses and their inhabitants were packed close together. There were maybe half a dozen single-family homes on our block. Most of us lived in semidetached or row houses.

Nicky lived in what was by far the biggest house on the corner of the block. It was white stucco with a walled-in patio and garden. A flower shop occupied the front half of the ground floor.

Nicky's father, Big Nick, ran the flower shop. He owned it actually. Big Nick did not look like the kind of guy who would be much interested in flowers; but then, Michelangelo didn't look like the kind of guy whose soul drove him to create such great beauty. So who knew? The difference was that I'd never actually seen Big Nick touch a flower, except to snap off its stem and stick the bud into the lapel of his jacket. And while it was pretty clear that everybody thought that being a florist was kind of a sissy job, I never heard anybody tease Big Nick about it, or about anything else for that matter. So I never did either. Besides, Big Nick was always real nice to us kids. He liked to pass out candy and, on special occasions, even dollar bills.

Little Nicky, on the other hand, did not seem to have inherited his father's magnanimous nature. Little Nicky was a loose cannon with a short fuse. You never knew what he was going to do next. Half the time he didn't know either. So being able to play with Nicky was a real test of one's mettle.

One of his favorite gags was dropping his frog, Nunzio, down someone's shirt. Carla Moretti was really the only one who panicked more than neurotic, little Nunzio. Then there was the time that Nicky ate a night crawler and Crazy Carla threw up. I have to admit, it took real intestinal fortitude on my part to keep my dinner down through that one. I just kept smiling and swallowing. I would not give Nicky the satisfaction of seeing me crack. That was his game after all. Nothing gave him greater pleasure than knowing that he'd found someone's breaking point.

But it was one day when he wasn't even trying that he finally found mine.

It was a perfect summer day right after fourth grade. I'd decided I was in the mood for a baseball game. So I got my glove and headed for Nicky's house. All baseball games, like everything else that went on in the neighborhood, were organized through Nicky. I went through the garden gate, around back to the family entrance, and rang the bell.

Nicky opened the door, took one look at me, and practically slammed the door in my face.

"Hey!" I pushed back.

"Go away," he told me.

I stuck my foot in the door like an unwanted salesman. "What's wrong with you?"

"I can't play with you anymore," he told me through the crack in the doorway.

I snickered. "What did you do now?" I prodded, thinking that his mother had grounded him again.

"Nothing," he said defensively.

"Then why can't you play?"

"I just can't, okay?"

"No, it's not okay," I told him. "I'm not going away until you tell me why."

"Because the guys are here."

I didn't see the problem. "Great! Let's go to the empty lot and play ball."

"That's what we were going to do."

"Well then, let's go," I insisted.

"You're not invited."

"Says who?"

"Everybody."

"Why?"

"Because you're a girl. You have cooties."

"You're a human cootie and we all play with you."

"Good thing you're a girl, or I'd beat you up."

"Why don't you come out here and try it." I put up my fists, left one high to protect my face.

"I don't hit girls," he said, condescendingly.

"Since when?" He'd rid me of a "baby" molar two weeks earlier when I'd dropped my left. The tooth fairy brought me a dollar and a quarter for that tooth. A quarter from my mother, who told me that the tooth fairy really wouldn't think that I deserved anything for losing a tooth in a fight. And a buck from the old man, who was glowing with pride.

"I don't hit girls," he reiterated, even more solicitously. "And I don't play with them. Face it, you're a girl and you have cooties."

I stood there dumbfounded. What else could I do? I wasn't allowed to cry. And Nicky wouldn't come out into the open where I could get a good shot at him.

When I finally turned to leave, Nicky slammed the door behind me. I walked away from the house, fighting to maintain my composure. When I got around to the front of the house, out on the pavement where I was pretty sure Nicky wouldn't be able to see me, I started to run for home. I heard myself panting as I ran and I heard a few whimpers escape. Rejected by Little Nicky Santucci! What worse indignities could one be forced to suffer in this life?

When I got home, my mother was in the kitchen so I managed to sneak past her. I went upstairs where I could be alone in my misery. All the frustration and rage I felt came pouring out. In no time at all, I was climbing the walls. I was literally climbing the walls. I did that to relieve pressure.

There was a section of hallway upstairs that was long and narrow, and when I braced myself with one hand and one foot against each wall, I could shimmy up. Then I could pace the hallway up near the ceiling. The trick was turning around. It was best to do that at the end of the hallway so that there was the third wall—over the door, of course—to use for balance.